ROM

Amazing
Grace!

A Guided Discovery for Groups and Individuals

Kevin Perrotta

LOYOLAPRESS.
A JESUIT MINISTRY
Chicago

LOYOLA PRESS.
A JESUIT MINISTRY

3441 N. Ashland Avenue
Chicago, Illinois 60657
(800) 621-1008
www.loyolapress.com

Nihil Obstat
Reverend Robert L. Schoenstene, S.S.L.
Censor Deputatus
February 14, 2005

Imprimatur
Reverend George J. Rassas
Vicar General
Archdiocese of Chicago
February 16, 2005

The *Nihil Obstat* and *Imprimatur* are official declarations that a book is free of doctrinal and moral error. No implication is contained therein that those who have granted the *Nihil Obstat* and *Imprimatur* agree with the content, opinions, or statements expressed. Nor do they assume any legal responsibility associated with publication.

The Scripture quotations contained herein are from the New Revised Standard Version Bible: Catholic Edition, copyright © 1993 and 1989 by the Division of Christian Education of the National Council of the Churches of Christ in the U.S.A. Used by permission. All rights reserved. Subheadings in Scripture quotations have been added by Kevin Perrotta.

The Catechism excerpts are from the English translation of the *Catechism of the Catholic Church* for use in the United States of America, Second Edition, copyright © 1994, 1997, United States Catholic Conference, Inc. – Libreria Editrice Vaticana. Used with permission.

Prayer by Blessed Charles de Foucauld (p. 74) is taken from *Écrits spirituels*, edited by de Gigord. The French text may be found in Robert Claude, S.J., and José Feder, S.J., eds., *Prie dans le secret* (Brussels: Casterman, 1966), 196. Translation by Louise Perrotta.

The excerpt from George T. Montague, S.M., (p. 75) is taken from *Riding the Wind: Learning the Ways of the Spirit* (Ann Arbor, MI: Word of Life/Servant Books, 1974), 44–47.

Prayer by St. Pio of Pietrelcina (p. 86) is excerpted from the version posted at the Internet site www.monksofadoration.org.

Interior design by Kay Hartmann/Communique Design
Illustration by Anni Betts

ISBN-13: 978-0-8294-2141-5; ISBN-10: 0-8294-2141-6

Printed in the United States of America
09 10 11 12 13 14 Bang 10 9 8 7 6 5 4 3 2

Contents

How to Use This Guide

You might compare the Bible to a national park. The park is so large that you could spend months, even years, getting to know it. But a brief visit, if carefully planned, can be enjoyable and worthwhile. In a few hours you can drive through the park and pull over at a handful of sites. At each stop you can get out of the car, take a short trail through the woods, listen to the wind blowing through the trees, get a feel for the place.

In this booklet, we will read excerpts from Paul's letter to the Christians of Rome. Because the excerpts are short, we will be able to take a leisurely walk through them, thinking carefully about what we are reading and what it means for our lives today.

This guide provides everything you need to explore Romans in six discussions—or to do a six-part exploration on your own. The introduction on page 6 will prepare you to get the most out of your reading. The weekly sections provide explanations that will help illuminate the meanings of the readings for your life. Equally important, each section supplies questions that will launch your group into fruitful discussion, helping you to both investigate Paul's letter for yourself and learn from one another. If you're using the booklet by yourself, the questions will spur your personal reflection.

Each discussion is meant to be a *guided discovery*.

Guided. None of us is equipped to read the Bible without help. We read the Bible *for* ourselves but not *by* ourselves. Scripture was written to be understood and applied in the community of faith. So each week "A Guide to the Reading," drawing on the work of both modern biblical scholars and Christian writers of the past, supplies background and explanations. The guide will help you grasp the meanings of the letter to the Romans. Think of it as a friendly park ranger who points out noteworthy details and explains what you're looking at so you can appreciate things for yourself.

Discovery. The purpose is for *you* to interact with Romans. "Questions for Careful Reading" is a tool to help you dig into the text and examine it carefully. "Questions for Application" will help you consider what these words mean for your life here and now. Each week concludes with an "Approach to Prayer" section that helps you respond to God's word. Supplementary "Living Tradition" and "Saints in the Making" sections offer the thoughts and experiences of Christians past and present. By showing what the letter has meant to others, these sections will help you consider what it means for you.

How long are the discussion sessions? We've assumed you will have about an hour and a half when you get together. If you have less time, you'll find that most of the elements can be shortened somewhat.

Is homework necessary? You will get the most out of your discussions if you read the weekly material and prepare your answers to the questions in advance of each meeting. If participants are not able to prepare, have someone read the "Guide to the Reading" sections aloud to the group at the points where they appear.

What about leadership? If you happen to have a world-class biblical scholar in your group, by all means ask him or her to lead the discussions. In the absence of any professional Scripture scholars, or even accomplished amateur biblical scholars, you can still have a first-class Bible discussion. Choose two or three people to take turns as facilitators, and have everyone read "Suggestions for Bible Discussion Groups" (page 90) before beginning.

Does everyone need a guide? a Bible? Everyone in the group will need his or her own copy of this booklet. It contains all the excerpts from Romans discussed in the weekly sessions, so a Bible is not absolutely necessary—but each participant will find it useful to have one. You should have at least one Bible on hand for your discussions (see page 92 for recommendations.)

How do we get started? Before you begin, take a look at the suggestions for Bible discussion groups (page 92) or individuals (page 95).

S itting in the sun-drenched courtyard of a friend's villa in the Greek city of Corinth around the year 56, the apostle Paul dictated a letter to some Christians he had never met, in the imperial capital, Rome. The believers were a small group living in a huge city awash in pagan religions and ruled by a corrupt elite. Paul sent them encouragement. "I'm proud of the gospel of Jesus Christ!" he declared. "I'm confident in God's power working through Jesus. You can be confident in it, too!"

Paul's letter was a communication between martyrs-to-be. As he wrote, Paul was about to set out on a trip to Jerusalem. There he would be attacked by a mob and jailed as a troublemaker. After a few years of imprisonment, perhaps in the year 61, he would be transported to stand trial in Rome—giving him the opportunity to meet the recipients of his letter. In Rome, he would eventually be executed, possibly in the year 67. In the meantime, in the year 64, the emperor Nero launched a vicious persecution of Christians in the city, sweeping some of Paul's readers to a gruesome death.

But Paul's letter was not swept away. Survivors of the persecution copied it and distributed it to Christians in other places. Recognizing the letter as an inspired statement of faith in Jesus, the early Christians eventually incorporated it into the New Testament.

The enduring value of Paul's letter stems from the fact that he put more into it than a few words of encouragement. The letter to the Romans is the longest of Paul's letters. The length has something to do with Paul's having some additional travel plans in mind. He was hoping, after his trip to Jerusalem, to visit the Christians in Rome and get their help for a missionary journey to Spain. To smooth the way for his visit, he composed a letter that would help them get to know him.

In other cities Paul had visited, his version of the gospel— the good news about Jesus—had met with criticism by some Christians (see his letter to the Galatians). The criticisms would have reached the ears of the believers in Rome. If Paul expected them to welcome him, he needed to clear up misunderstandings beforehand. So he devoted much of his letter to laying out the gospel as he preached it. He focused on issues where the Roman Christians might have questions about his thinking.

Sitting in his friend's house in Corinth, Paul poured into the letter his deepest reflections on who Jesus is and what he means for men and women. The result was the most carefully composed statement of faith by Paul or any other leader of the Church in the age of the apostles. The letter flashes with the enthusiasm and hope of a man who has spent years pondering the gospel, sharing it with other people, and observing its effects in their lives—a man who was headed toward martyrdom for his preaching about Jesus.

Paul focuses on the points he thinks are most important for the Romans to understand, without explaining the whole background of his thinking. He leaves many assumptions unstated. Much of what he assumed may have been obvious to his readers in Rome. But some of his assumptions are not entirely familiar to us, so we may have some difficulty following his presentation. Before we begin to read, then, it will be useful to look at some of what Paul says in Romans and some things he does not say in the letter, in order to grasp his view of the condition of the world and of where the human race stands in relation to God.

As a Jew, Paul believes that one God created all that is. God made the human race in his own image, with the desire that we would reflect his goodness and love—his "glory" as Paul would say. Indeed, God formed us as the apex of creation: we are the part of creation capable of knowing and loving him. In us, creation becomes able to recognize God's goodness, to thank and praise him, to freely serve him. The rest of creation is to be the material with which we carry out this mission.

Given this arrangement, human disobedience to God would be a cosmic disaster. If humans were to refuse to live out their role of praise and obedience toward God, we and the rest of creation would be thrown into disorder. Were we to turn away from the life-giving God, we would set ourselves on a course toward darkness and death. We would disfigure ourselves, losing our likeness to God. The rest of creation would be reduced to futility, blocked from playing its role as the instrument by which we enter into communion with God.

It goes without saying that this is precisely the disaster into which humans plunged themselves. The first human beings sinned. Adam and Eve's disobedience to God wrecked the order within and between them: they experienced guilt and shame; they became jealous, fearful, irresponsible, and domineering. They shattered the harmony between themselves and the rest of creation. Indeed, the rest of creation was damaged by their turning away from God. As you probably know, all this can be found in the first three chapters of the Bible.

Paul views the first human couple not only as our ancestors but as our representatives. Thus, their decision to disobey God had consequences for those who came after them. By abandoning God, they not only damaged themselves; they passed on human nature in a damaged condition to all of us.

In addition, our first parents' rebellion against God left them vulnerable to the power of evil spiritual forces that are in rebellion against him. Adam and Eve's sin gave these evil spiritual powers a bridgehead in human society. From it, they seek to extend their deceptive and destructive influence over all of us.

Given the kind of world we are born into, and the kind of people we are from birth, it is no surprise that each of us adds our own sins to the ongoing disaster in which we find ourselves.

But God loved human beings no less after we sinned than before. As soon as our first parents turned away from him, he began to unfold a plan to lead us back to himself. This plan worked through a particular Near Eastern people—the people of Israel—whom God gathered, brought into a covenant with himself, and instructed in his way of life. This instruction is known as the law of Moses, since Moses was the man through whom God gave the instruction. Paul refers to it simply as "the law."

Jews view this covenant and law as God's definitive action toward the human race. For much of his life, Paul shared this conviction. By the time he writes to the Romans, however, he has come to regard the Mosaic law as a stopgap measure undertaken by God in preparation for his truly definitive action—the coming of his Son.

On the basis of God's promises in the Scriptures, many Jews in Paul's day expected that God was eventually going to bring the present age of history to an end and replace it with a better situation. They expected God to show his righteousness, that is, to save the oppressed, vindicate those who obeyed him, and bring judgment on those who disobeyed him. God's intervention, many Jews thought, would be preceded by severe disturbances in the world, tribulations of various kinds. Some Jews expected a divinely appointed agent—"Messiah" in Hebrew, "Christos" in Greek—to lead God's forces to victory over sin and evil. The dead would be raised up. Justice and peace would be permanently established. In short, God would bring his kingdom.

Years before he wrote to the Romans, Paul received a vision while traveling on the road between Jerusalem and Damascus. (If you get the impression that Paul was constantly traveling, you are correct. He was one of the great travelers of the first century.) The vision convinced him that God had begun to fulfill the expectations of the Jewish people through Jesus of Nazareth. Jesus is the Messiah. His crucifixion was the beginning of the final turmoil and suffering that were to afflict the world when God's kingdom began to arrive. Jesus' rising from the tomb was the beginning of the resurrection from the dead. The revelation of God's righteousness in the world had now begun: God was bringing sin under judgment, overthrowing the evil spiritual powers at work in human society, setting his creation to rights. Through Jesus, God offered men and women forgiveness of sins and a share in his life through the Holy Spirit. The new order was already entering our disordered world. Ultimately, God would complete the coming of his kingdom by recreating all things through his Son. Those who believed in him would rise to life with God forever.

Jewish people in Paul's time expected that God's end-time action would affect not only themselves but the other peoples of the world, also. Paul saw the fulfillment of this expectation also in Jesus. Jesus is the path that God has provided to himself, not only for Jews but also for non-Jews—"gentiles." Thus the Mosaic law, Paul concluded, which lies at the heart of God's special relationship with the Jewish people, is no longer the best framework for people's relationship with God. Instead, God offers everyone a direct relationship with himself through faith in Jesus and the gift of his Holy Spirit.

Where does this leave the people of Israel? What place, if any, does the Mosaic law continue to have in people's relationship with God? These were urgent questions for both Jews and gentiles in Paul's day. Answering them was one of his main goals in the letter to the Romans.

While Paul wrote especially for Roman Christians in the mid-first century, his letter contains so much insight into the mystery of Christ that it has crackled with excitement for every later generation of believers. Paul speaks about the frustrations of struggling against sin, about our need for God's grace, about God's merciful, fatherly love, about the splendor of life with Christ. His words have not lost any of their freshness in the twenty centuries since Paul's first readers in first-century Rome gathered in their homes to listen to them.

Nevertheless, Paul is not an easy writer to understand. From his own day until ours, readers have had to work to grasp his meaning (2 Peter 3:15–16). Apparently, people did not always find Paul easy to understand even when he spoke to them face to face (this seems to be implied in 2 Thessalonians 2:5). Even in his letter to the Romans, where Paul is working to clear up misunderstandings, his presentation is sometimes difficult to follow. We cannot entirely blame Paul for this, since his subject matter is deep and complex. In any case, it is up to us to make our best effort to discover his meaning. The Guides to the Reading will aid your understanding. But let me give you a heads-up here about one source of difficulty.

Some of the terms that Paul employs have a wealth of biblical precedent behind them. If we want to grasp what he is saying, we have to do some homework in the Old Testament. The leading example of this is the package of terms that are usually translated into English as *righteousness, righteous, justice, just, justify, justified,* and *justification* (all these English words translate words in Paul's letter that come from a single root word in the Greek language). We tend to think of justice as something having to do with a courtroom. And we tend to think of justice as distinct from, even contrary to, mercy. But Paul is working with a concept shaped by the Old Testament, where *righteousness,* or *justice,* has a somewhat different range of meanings.

In the Old Testament, the Hebrew word often translated "righteousness" or "justice" concerns doing what is right toward other people, relating to them with loyalty, not just in court but in ordinary life. God shows his righteousness by relating to his people with loyalty and saving people from enemies and oppressors. A good example—worth careful reading before one begins to explore Romans—is Isaiah 51:1–8. There the same Hebrew word is translated (in the NRSV) both "righteousness" (Isaiah 51:1, 7) and "deliverance" (Isaiah 51:5, 6, 8).

In the Bible, righteousness is not opposed to mercy but includes it. A righteous person is kind and willing to forgive; a person who lacks compassion is not truly righteous. This connection of righteousness with mercy is reflected in Jesus' parable in which a man who refuses to show mercy is called "wicked" (Matthew 18:32). This connection explains why people in the Old Testament appeal to God's righteousness when they ask him for forgiveness. Obviously, his righteousness includes mercy, since it is mercy and kindness, not "strict justice," that would incline him to forgive. A good example of the connection of justice and mercy, also worth careful reading if you wish to understand Romans, is Psalm 143. Notice how (in the NRSV) "righteousness" (Psalm 143:11) is virtually a synonym for "steadfast love" (Psalm 143:12).

As you will see, a further challenge in understanding Paul is that he uses some words with shifting meanings. As the Guides to the Reading will point out, key terms such as *flesh, body, law,* and *sin* have different meanings at different stages in Paul's presentation. So stay alert!

THERE'S GOOD NEWS AND BAD NEWS

Questions to Begin

15 minutes
Use a question or two to get warmed up for the reading.

1 Who would you most like to visit, if you could?

2 Who would you most like to pay you a visit?

5 minutes
Read the passage aloud. Let individuals take turns reading sections.

The Reading: Romans 1

From: Paul. To: Roman Christians. Re: Jesus Christ.

1:1 Paul, a servant of Jesus Christ, called to be an apostle, set apart for the gospel of God, 2 which he promised beforehand through his prophets in the holy scriptures, 3 the gospel concerning his Son, who was descended from David according to the flesh 4 and was declared to be Son of God with power according to the spirit of holiness by resurrection from the dead, Jesus Christ our Lord, 5 through whom we have received grace and apostleship to bring about the obedience of faith among all the Gentiles for the sake of his name, 6 including yourselves who are called to belong to Jesus Christ,

7 To all God's beloved in Rome, who are called to be saints:
Grace to you and peace from God our Father and the Lord Jesus Christ.

It Would Be Great to Visit

8 First, I thank my God through Jesus Christ for all of you, because your faith is proclaimed throughout the world. 9 For God, whom I serve with my spirit by announcing the gospel of his Son, is my witness that without ceasing I remember you always in my prayers, 10 asking that by God's will I may somehow at last succeed in coming to you. 11 For I am longing to see you so that I may share with you some spiritual gift to strengthen you— 12 or rather so that we may be mutually encouraged by each other's faith, both yours and mine. 13 I want you to know, brothers and sisters, that I have often intended to come to you (but thus far have been prevented), in order that I may reap some harvest among you as I have among the rest of the Gentiles. 14 I am a debtor both to Greeks and to barbarians, both to the wise and to the foolish 15 —hence my eagerness to proclaim the gospel to you also who are in Rome.

The Message in a Nutshell

16 For I am not ashamed of the gospel; it is the power of God for salvation to everyone who has faith, to the Jew first and also to the Greek. 17 For in it the righteousness of God is revealed through faith for faith; as it is written, "The one who is righteous will live by faith."

It's a Jungle Out There

18 For the wrath of God is revealed from heaven against all ungodliness and wickedness of those who by their wickedness suppress the truth.

19 For what can be known about God is plain to them, because God has shown it to them. 20 Ever since the creation of the world his eternal power and divine nature, invisible though they are, have been understood and seen through the things he has made. So they are without excuse; 21 for though they knew God, they did not honor him as God or give thanks to him, but they became futile in their thinking, and their senseless minds were darkened. 22 Claiming to be wise, they became fools; 23 and they exchanged the glory of the immortal God for images resembling a mortal human being or birds or four-footed animals or reptiles.

24 Therefore God gave them up in the lusts of their hearts to impurity, to the degrading of their bodies among themselves, 25 because they exchanged the truth about God for a lie and worshiped and served the creature rather than the Creator, who is blessed forever! Amen.

26 For this reason God gave them up to degrading passions. Their women exchanged natural intercourse for unnatural, 27 and in the same way also the men, giving up natural intercourse with women, were consumed with passion for one another. Men committed shameless acts with men and received in their own persons the due penalty for their error.

28 And since they did not see fit to acknowledge God, God gave them up to a debased mind and to things that should not be done. 29 They were filled with every kind of wickedness, evil, covetousness, malice. Full of envy, murder, strife, deceit, craftiness, they are gossips, 30 slanderers, God-haters, insolent, haughty, boastful, inventors of evil, rebellious toward parents, 31 foolish, faithless, heartless, ruthless.

32 They know God's decree, that those who practice such things deserve to die—yet they not only do them but even applaud others who practice them.

Questions for Careful Reading

1 *Romans 1*

10 minutes
Choose questions according to your interest and time.

1 What indications does Paul give in 1:1–7 (unless noted, all biblical citations in this book refer to Romans) that God laid plans long ago for what is now happening in the lives of Paul and the Christians in Rome?

2 What might Paul mean by the term "obedience of faith" (1:5)?

3 Paul seems to correct himself in 1:11–12. Why?

4 In 1:8–15, what signs does Paul give indicating he perceives that God is in control of his life?

5 From statements Paul makes in 1:18–32, what does he mean by *acknowledging* God (see 1:28)? What does it mean to acknowledge God?

6 Speaking about people who turned away from God, Paul says, "God gave them up" (1:24, 26, 28). What did God give them up to?

A Guide to the Reading

If participants have not read this section already, read it aloud. Otherwise go on to "Questions for Application."

1:1–7. Verses 1–7 form one long, dense sentence—not an easy start for the reader! This opening sentence alerts us to the fact that Paul's writing will require slow and patient reading.

1:8–17. Paul discusses his intentions to visit the Roman Christians (1:8–15). But it quickly becomes clear that he is not writing a chatty letter about personal affairs. This letter is going to be serious theological business. Verses 16 and 17 contain Paul's message in a nutshell. Here, every word counts.

◆ "Salvation." Paul means getting successfully through the challenges of earthly life in a way that pleases God, receiving a favorable evaluation of one's life by God at the final judgment, and entering into the permanent joy of God's kingdom.

◆ "The power of God for salvation." Paul is not speaking mainly about who God is but about what he has done. The gospel—literally "good news"—is the announcement that God has acted powerfully through the death and resurrection of Jesus of Nazareth. The message comes with an invitation to experience God's action—an invitation that God drives home powerfully in our minds and hearts. To accept the invitation is to open ourselves up to God's power.

◆ "The righteousness of God is revealed." It might sound as though Paul is saying that a curtain in heaven has been pulled aside, allowing us to look up and see that God is just. But Paul means that God is showing his righteousness by operating down here in our human world. God has begun to set things right, to save all who need to be saved, to put an end to evil in every form.

◆ "Through faith for faith." From beginning to end, faith in God is the key to the lifelong process of receiving and cooperating with his powerful action.

1:18–32. Whoa! What happened to the good news? From verse 18 on, the news is pretty grim. Sometimes my wife tells me to put down the newspaper because it is making me depressed. She would probably prefer that I skip over this part of Romans.

Here, Paul begins a lengthy explanation, which continues in the following chapters. The beginning will make more sense when we get the full picture. Paul's purpose is not to paint the world in the darkest possible colors—and certainly not to make us depressed—but to set the stage for his presentation of the gospel. By reminding us of our sins, he helps us see where we need to experience God's power.

It may seem strange that Paul follows his statement about God revealing his power to save with the declaration that "the wrath of God is revealed" (1:18). But God's saving action inevitably has a negative dimension. Setting the world right means confronting everything that is taking the world in the wrong direction. In order to save his creation from the human ingratitude, selfishness, and injustice that mar it, God must bring the forces of evil—and those who perpetrate it—under judgment. Destruction and loss are inevitable. Emancipating slaves, for example, involves despoiling slave owners. This destruction and loss are the downside of God's action, and they are on full display in verses 18–32.

Paul sees a pattern of human pride and divine judgment. To make the pattern obvious, he describes it three times (1:21–24, 25–27, and 28–31; the pattern is obscured by the punctuation in the translation). It is a three-step pattern: (1) When people turn away from God (1:21–23, 25, and 28), (2) God hands them over to their own desires (1:24, 26, and 28), and (3) people then degrade themselves in various sins (1:24, 26–27, and 28–31).

It is important to avoid a misunderstanding concerning the term "wrath" here. This "wrath" is the fatal effect of rejecting God, the doom to which sin leads, the justified punishment that sin incurs. Think of sin as poison and "wrath" as its fatal effect. It is *God's* wrath in the sense that God, being utterly opposed to the abuse of his good creation by sin, is determined that those who sin will suffer its consequences. This wrath is *not* personal anger. Paul is not saying that God is angry at people. If God can be said to be angry at all, he is angry at *sin;* but, as Paul will explain, God is almost incredibly compassionate toward *sinners.* Out of his infinite love, God has rescued us from the dreadful consequences of our sins. Indeed, God hopes that our experience of wrath will spur us to return to him.

Verses 18–32 are sometimes cited as a warning about the judgment that will befall a society where sin prevails. But notice that Paul does not say that *sin* leads to *punishment;* he says that *refusal to acknowledge God* leads to *sin.* When we refuse to acknowledge God, our minds become darkened; God then reveals his "wrath" by letting us wander off into the evils we choose. "If it's sin you want," God says, "sin you may have."

Paul believes that at the Last Judgment God will bring a punishment on sin. But he indicates that in the present world a punishment already follows sin. God's judgment on our abandonment of him is to give us the freedom to do what we want. This may seem an odd form of punishment, since we generally think of punishment as the imposition of something that we do not want, something that goes against our will. But Paul assumes that sin is inherently harmful; it inevitably has painful consequences. Even if the external ill effects of our sins are, for a while, hard to detect, being dominated by our own desires—controlled by lust (1:24), "consumed with passion" (1:27)—is a miserable, "degrading" state to be in (1:24, 26). It involves a loss of our true humanity, a twisting and crippling of our personalities. Sin makes us "foolish, faithless, heartless, ruthless" (1:31). What could be worse than that?

When did this pattern of rejecting God and being delivered into sin occur? Is Paul thinking of an event (a) at the beginning of human existence, with Adam and Eve? (b) that goes on repeatedly in societies through history? (c) that happens in each of our lives? Possibly (d) all of the above.

Paul states that God reveals himself to all people through the universe he has created (1:19–20). But pagan religions that regard nature as semidivine (1:22–23) fail to accurately perceive God. Elsewhere, Paul indicates that pagan religions have positive features (Acts 14:16; 17:22–31). Here, however, his treatment is entirely negative because he wishes to underline the point that there is an element of pride in humans' refusal to recognize and honor God (1:21), a tendency to think that we are wiser than we are (1:22). Obviously, this can be a problem for Christians as well as others.

In addition, Paul says, people have an innate knowledge of right and wrong; "they know God's decree," without special revelation (1:32). Paul mentions this moral knowledge after he has listed various vices that people fall into, so apparently he believes that we still know something about right and wrong even when our minds become darkened by pride and sin (see 2:14–15). Sin does not result in total ignorance of good but produces a state of bad conscience: we fail to live the truth that we at least dimly recognize.

Paul characterizes human beings as both knowing and being confused about God and morality—an accurate picture, most of us would say. Is he criticizing human reason (1:22)? Not at all. He thinks that our reason is good but that our thinking goes off in wrong directions as soon as we begin to ignore God. Does Paul have a low view of the human body? On the contrary, sin is bad because it dishonors the body (1:24).

Paul makes rather a big deal of homosexual activity (1:26–27). One scholar, Brendan Byrne, S.J., explains that Paul focuses on it not because it was a pressing pastoral problem among Christians of his day (it wasn't) but because Jews of his day considered pagans' easy acceptance of homosexual practice as a particularly clear example of the kind of moral confusion that paganism can lead to. Paul does not offer an explanation of the origins of homosexuality, any more than he charts the genesis of the other problems he mentions here.

Paul has written this section (1:18–32) as though he is having a conversation with a fellow Jew. Paul and his friend look around at the gentile world and remark on all the idolatry and sin out there. "Yup, that's the gentile world for you," Paul's friend may be thinking at the end of the reading. But if the observation of others' sins makes the friend feel morally complacent—well, just wait for next week's reading.

Questions for Application

40 minutes
Choose questions according to your interest and time.

1 In 1:1–7 Paul speaks of himself and the Roman Christians being called by God. How have you experienced God's call? Who has God called you to serve? How is your way of relating with the people in your life shaped by your sense of being called by God?

2 Reread 1:7. Are you called to be a saint? What are you doing about it?

3 How have you experienced the power of God's word? Are you willing to open yourself to God's power? How could you express your openness to God?

4 Paul speaks of a connection between resisting God and failing to understand life (1:18–32). When have you experienced this connection?

5 Where in your life do you find it difficult to acknowledge God? What would help?

6 Give an example of how acknowledging God might require a person to act contrary to social expectations. Where might God be calling you to do this?

7 How is society affected when people acknowledge God? when people fail to acknowledge God? Identify an area of society where there seems to be a lack of acknowledgment of God: what consequences does this have for people's lives?

8 Paul speaks of sin as an obstacle to our becoming the persons God created us to be. How has obedience to God contributed to your becoming a person you and God can be happy with?

9 For personal reflection: How have your sins prevented you from becoming the person God intends you to be? What negative consequences have you seen from your sins? Where would repentance in your life now open the way for constructive change? What step do you need to take?

You must bring your personal needs to the reading. Whether you hunger for growth, self-understanding, peace, refreshment, or challenge, the Bible exists to meet personal hungers.

H. A. Nielsen, *The Bible—As If for the First Time*

Approach to Prayer

♦ Pray Psalm 143 together. Let individuals take turns reading the verses from whichever translations they may have. Pause for silent reflection. End together with an Our Father.

Saints in the Making

Finding Faith in an Unexpected Place

This section is a supplement for individual reading.

I am longing to see you so that I may share with you some spiritual gift to strengthen you—or rather so that we may be mutually encouraged by each other's faith (Romans 1:11–12).

By Al O'Brien

It's easy to lose hope on death row. Prisoners are in their cells twenty-three and a half hours a day. The average stay on death row is ten years. During the time Donald Aldrich was on death row, he went through a period of deep despair. He gave away anything with a Christian connection. When I first visited him, I told him not to feel stressed out about that. Most of the great saints have been through a period of desolation. By the time the date of his execution arrived, he had made a full recovery in his faith.

I spent the last hour with Don before his death. I read John 17 to him—the prayer that Christ prayed before he was executed. We prayed the Divine Mercy Chaplet together. We talked and shared and cried a little bit. He received Our Lord in the Eucharist, and I blessed him. Don had confidence and hope in the face of what he *knew* was going to happen to him in an hour. When the time came, he asked forgiveness of those he had hurt and told the warden he was ready. After he died, his body was removed to a local funeral home where I gave him a final blessing. His body was still warm to my touch.

Don left behind a poem that began: "We pray to thee, Lord Jesus, / Convict our hearts and seize us, / On knee our sins we will confess, / Our lives we ask You now to bless."

I have witnessed six executions. It always takes me a long time to process what I've been involved with—the intentional taking of a life. But I have seen what grace can do in preparing a person for death and the serenity it can produce. Truly, I believe what Christ said to St. Paul: "My grace is sufficient for you" (2 Corinthians 12:9).

Deacon Al O'Brien directs the criminal justice ministry in the diocese of Beaumont, Texas. Donald L. Aldrich was executed in Beaumont on October 12, 2004. The Catholic Church condemns capital punishment under circumstances in which society can be protected by other means; see the *Catechism of the Catholic Church*, section 2267.

HUMANITY IN A DEAD END

Questions to Begin

15 minutes
Use a question or two to get warmed up for the reading.

1   When you get lost on the
road, do you stop and ask for
directions?

2   Describe a situation where you
find it difficult to be impartial
and fair.

Opening the Bible

5 minutes
*Read the passage aloud. Let individuals take turns reading
paragraphs.*

The Reading: Romans 1:18–24, 28–31; 2:1–29; 3:9–26

Back to Last Week's Reading: Gentiles Sin

1:18 For the wrath of God is revealed from heaven against all ungodliness and wickedness of those who by their wickedness suppress the truth.
19 For what can be known about God is plain to them, because God has shown it to them. 20 Ever since the creation of the world his eternal power and divine nature, invisible though they are, have been understood and seen through the things he has made. So they are without excuse; 21 for though they knew God, they did not honor him as God or give thanks to him, but they became futile in their thinking, and their senseless minds were darkened. 22 Claiming to be wise, they became fools; 23 and they exchanged the glory of the immortal God for images resembling a mortal human being or birds or four-footed animals or reptiles.
24 Therefore God gave them up in the lusts of their hearts to impurity, to the degrading of their bodies among themselves. . . .
28 And since they did not see fit to acknowledge God, God gave them up to a debased mind and to things that should not be done. 29 They were filled with every kind of wickedness, evil, covetousness, malice. Full of envy, murder, strife, deceit, craftiness, they are gossips, 30 slanderers, God-haters, insolent, haughty, boastful, inventors of evil, rebellious toward parents, 31 foolish, faithless, heartless, ruthless.

Jews Also Sin

2:1 Therefore you have no excuse, whoever you are, when you judge others; for in passing judgment on another you condemn yourself, because you, the judge, are doing the very same things. 2 You say, "We know that God's judgment on those who do such things is in accordance with truth." 3 Do you imagine, whoever you are, that when you judge those who do such things and yet do them yourself, you will escape the judgment of God? 4 Or do you despise the riches of his kindness and forbearance and patience? Do you not realize that God's kindness is meant to lead you to repentance?

5 But by your hard and impenitent heart you are storing up wrath for yourself on the day of wrath, when God's righteous judgment will be revealed. 6 For he will repay according to each one's deeds: 7 to those who by patiently doing good seek for glory and honor and immortality, he will give eternal life; 8 while for those who are self-seeking and who obey not the truth but wickedness, there will be wrath and fury. 9 There will be anguish and distress for everyone who does evil, the Jew first and also the Greek, 10 but glory and honor and peace for everyone who does good, the Jew first and also the Greek. 11 For God shows no partiality.

Gentiles Will Not Be at a Disadvantage on Judgment Day

12 All who have sinned apart from the law will also perish apart from the law, and all who have sinned under the law will be judged by the law. 13 For it is not the hearers of the law who are righteous in God's sight, but the doers of the law who will be justified. 14 When Gentiles, who do not possess the law, do instinctively what the law requires, these, though not having the law, are a law to themselves. 15 They show that what the law requires is written on their hearts, to which their own conscience also bears witness; and their conflicting thoughts will accuse or perhaps excuse them 16 on the day when, according to my gospel, God, through Jesus Christ, will judge the secret thoughts of all.

Knowledge Is No Substitute for Action

17 But if you call yourself a Jew and rely on the law and boast of your relation to God 18 and know his will and determine what is best because you are instructed in the law, 19 and if you are sure that you are a guide to the blind, a light to those who are in darkness, 20 a corrector of the foolish, a teacher of children, having in the law the embodiment of knowledge and truth, 21 you, then, that teach others, will you not teach yourself? While you preach against stealing, do you steal? 22 You that forbid adultery, do you commit adultery? You that abhor idols, do you rob temples? 23 You that boast in the law, do you dishonor God by breaking the law? 24 For, as it is written, "The name of God is blasphemed among the Gentiles because of you."

Without Deeds, Religious Signs Are Valueless

25 Circumcision indeed is of value if you obey the law; but if you break the law, your circumcision has become uncircumcision. 26 So, if those who are uncircumcised keep the requirements of the law, will not their uncircumcision be regarded as circumcision? 27 Then those who are physically uncircumcised but keep the law will condemn you that have the written code and circumcision but break the law. 28 For a person is not a Jew who is one outwardly, nor is true circumcision something external and physical. 29 Rather, a person is a Jew who is one inwardly, and real circumcision is a matter of the heart—it is spiritual and not literal. Such a person receives praise not from others but from God.

In the End, Jews Will Have No Special Advantage

3:9 What then? Are we any better off? No, not at all; for we have already charged that all, both Jews and Greeks, are under the power of sin, 10 as it is written:
"There is no one who is righteous, not even one;
11 there is no one who has understanding,
there is no one who seeks God.
12 All have turned aside, together they have become
worthless;
there is no one who shows kindness,
there is not even one."
13 "Their throats are opened graves;
they use their tongues to deceive."
"The venom of vipers is under their lips."
14 "Their mouths are full of cursing and bitterness."
15 "Their feet are swift to shed blood;
16 ruin and misery are in their paths,
17 and the way of peace they have not known."
18 "There is no fear of God before their eyes."

19 Now we know that whatever the law says, it speaks to those who are under the law, so that every mouth may be silenced, and the whole world may be held accountable to God. 20 For "no human

being will be justified in his sight" by deeds prescribed by the law, for through the law comes the knowledge of sin.

God Has Brought Us out of Our Dead End

21 But now, apart from law, the righteousness of God has been disclosed, and is attested by the law and the prophets, 22 the righteousness of God through faith in Jesus Christ for all who believe. For there is no distinction, 23 since all have sinned and fall short of the glory of God; 24 they are now justified by his grace as a gift, through the redemption that is in Christ Jesus, 25 whom God put forward as a sacrifice of atonement by his blood, effective through faith. He did this to show his righteousness, because in his divine forbearance he had passed over the sins previously committed; 26 it was to prove at the present time that he himself is righteous and that he justifies the one who has faith in Jesus.

10 minutes
Choose questions according to your interest and time.

1 When have you seen an example of what Paul speaks of in 2:14?

2 Can you sort out the different meanings of "law" in 2:14?

3 Why is it *good* news—part of the "gospel"—that God will ultimately "judge the secret thoughts of all" (2:16)?

4 Is Paul criticizing the Mosaic law in 2:17–24? In 2:25–29, is he criticizing circumcision as a sign of a man's belonging to Judaism?

5 Paul speaks of the human race falling "short of the glory of God" (3:23). How might this statement be taken as a summary of the condition of humanity described in 1:18–32?

A Guide to the Reading

If participants have not read this section already, read it aloud. Otherwise go on to "Questions for Application."

2:1–16. Paul and his imaginary Jewish conversation partner have been standing side by side, shaking their heads as they look at all the sin out there in the pagan world (1:18–32). Now Paul turns to face his Jewish friend and says, "Therefore *you* have no excuse" (2:1; emphasis added). His friend is caught by surprise. *Why are you pointing a finger at me?* the friend wonders.

By leading his friend to sit in judgment on other people's sins, Paul has demonstrated that his friend knows a lot about right and wrong. So when the friend sins, he or she cannot plead ignorance (2:3). No doubt the very act of sitting in judgment on other people is wrong, but that is not Paul's point. He is accusing his friend of failing to meet the standards that he or she acknowledges and even teaches others (2:17–23).

Paul asks his Jewish friend whether he or she expects to be judged more leniently than others by God (2:3). Quite possibly the friend would answer yes: "We Jews have a privileged position with God as his chosen people. He does not punish us as our sins deserve. And since we avoid idolatry—the worst sin of all—we can expect favorable treatment at the final judgment." Some Old Testament writings might seem to support this view (Wisdom 12:22; 14; 15:1–3; 16:7–11). "That's a dangerous illusion!" Paul declares (2:4–5). God is impartial (2:11). He will not show favoritism at the Last Judgment but will judge every person on the basis of his or her behavior (2:6–10). Jews will be judged according to their obedience to the Mosaic law ("the law" in 2:12–13). Others will be judged according to their obedience to the law that God has "written on their hearts" (2:15).

2:17–29. Because the point is so important, and difficult for his friend to absorb, Paul insists that Jews cannot presume on God's favor. Paul does not find fault with the moral standards of Judaism but with the moral complacency of individual Jews.

The problem is not with the Mosaic law (2:13); the problem is being confident of God's favor because one possesses the law (or is "in the law," as Paul says literally in 3:19) even while failing to keep it. Paul's line of thinking is nothing new in Judaism. Long before his time, criticizing one another for unfaithfulness to God's law was a very Jewish thing to do. The prophet Jeremiah rebuked his fellow Jews for relying on the temple in Jerusalem to save them from the consequences of their sins (Jeremiah 7:1–10). He was not criticizing the temple but the misuse of the temple. (See also John the Baptist and Jesus—Luke 3:7–14; Matthew 23.) A person cannot rest secure in his or her relationship with God simply because of belonging to the Jewish people, Paul says; what counts with God is how you actually live. The same principle applies to everyone, of course, including Christians.

3:9–20. This raises the question as to whether there is any advantage in being Jewish. Paul's answer is a qualified yes. Jews have a privileged place at the center of God's action in the world (3:2; 9:4–5)—seats at the fifty-yard line, so to speak. It is obviously a benefit to know what God is about in the world. Yet those who fail to obey God will ultimately be no better off than anyone else (3:9).

In theory, the message of God's impartiality opens a door of hope to non-Jews, since *all* "who by patiently doing good seek for glory and honor and immortality" will receive eternal life (2:7). But did you notice that Paul never says that anyone actually *does* receive eternal life on this basis? And now he points to the sad fact about the world that he has been examining on and off ever since 1:18: everybody sins (3:9–18). The message of God's impartial judgment on the basis of our behavior turns out to be crushingly bad news. At the Last Judgment, "'no human being will be justified'" (3:20). In one way or another, we have fallen short of God's intentions.

No human being, Paul says, will be judged righteous by God "by deeds prescribed by the law" (3:20). Does Paul mean there is something wrong with what the Mosaic law prescribes? No, as Paul will make emphatically clear (chapter 7; 8:4). Does he mean there is something wrong with *trying* to follow God's law, as though, in a counterintuitive way, the human attempt to obey God is inherently misguided? Far from it; at the final judgment, "the doers of the law . . . will be justified" (2:13)—if there are any. Paul means that no one who takes the route of being "under the law" (3:19) will arrive at a final verdict of *righteous.* Life within the framework of the Mosaic law (also life within the framework of conscience) does not lead to righteousness, for the simple reason that the law prescribes what is right without empowering people to do it. Lacking the power, we do not consistently obey God.

So our goose is cooked. Only those who perfectly reflect God's goodness can enter his presence and enjoy his love forever. Alas, none of us will qualify.

3:21–26. Paul has declared that God is revealing his righteousness (1:17). This means not only that God is bringing judgment by letting us continue to sin and suffer the consequences (1:18–32) but also that he is rescuing. Above all, he is rescuing us from the oppression of our own sins. We cannot make ourselves qualified to be with God, so God has begun the process of making us qualified. Paul uses a rich vocabulary to communicate the immensity of Christ's action for us:

- ◆ We are "justified." Here, Paul uses a Greek legal term. He means that God acquits us, declares us innocent. The verdict is not a legal fiction, as if God decided to treat us as though we were righteous despite that fact that we remain as guilty as ever. Nor is the verdict a magical decree that instantly transforms us into perfect persons. God's verdict of "justified" means, first of all, that he forgives us—and more, as we will see.
- ◆ We receive "redemption." The Greek term comes from the sphere of slave owning in the ancient world. Freeing a slave or rescuing a captive was called "redemption." Sometimes, redemption meant paying a ransom to the slave owner, but not necessarily. What exactly Jesus has redeemed us *from* will also become clearer in the next few chapters.
- ◆ We experience "atonement." This word comes from the realm of sacrifices in the ancient world. It indicates that God removes our sins, rids us of guilt, annuls, cancels the punishment that our sins deserve, and gives us peace with him. Through Jesus' death for us, God reconciles us to himself.

Observe that Paul does not say that Jesus has turned God's anger away from us. There was no need for that, since God was not angry at us. Because of his deep compassion for us, God "put forward" his Son as the perfect agent for removing our sins. As the *Catechism of the Catholic Church* says, "By giving up his own Son for our sins, God manifests that his plan for us is one of benevolent love" (section 604).

God gave Jesus to us as "a sacrifice of atonement by his blood" (3:25). In Israelite religious thinking, blood equaled life. Jesus, in other words, brought us atonement by giving up his life willingly, dying in obedience to God's plan (see Mark 10:45; 14:32–42; John 10:17–18; 12:27–28; Philippians 2:8). The element of Jesus' *voluntary* submission to God is crucial, for through Jesus' obedience to death, God forgives our acts of disobedience and changes our disobedient hearts (more on this in chapter 5). How could Jesus' obedience blot out our disobedience? How could God love us so much as to give his Son to atone for us? How could the Son love us so much that he would embrace this plan? We are at the heart of very great mysteries here.

God has acted through Christ "apart from the law" (3:21), that is, outside the framework of the Mosaic law, where divine instruction encountered human incapacity to obey. Because God's action is outside the Mosaic law, it is available equally to gentiles and to Jews. A person does not need to be or become a Jew in order to benefit from what Jesus has accomplished by his death; one simply needs to recognize that Jesus' death is God's saving action and to be willing to respond. In other words, what is required is simple faith (3:22), which is accessible to those inside and those outside the Mosaic law.

By our sins, we have fallen short of God's glory (3:23). We have lost some of the resemblance to God that he created us to bear. Now, in Jesus, God has begun the process of restoring our resemblance to himself.

Questions for Application

40 minutes
Choose questions according to your interest and time.

1 When have you realized that your criticism of another person's failings could be applied also to yourself? What did you learn from this experience?

2 What sorts of excuses do people offer for their sins? What sorts of excuses do you use?

3 Reread 2:4. In your own life, or in the life of someone you know, when has one person's kindness and patience helped another person turn away from sin?

4 Reread 3:21–26. Mention an area of your life where Jesus' redeeming love has been important to you. (It doesn't have to be your deepest, darkest area of sin!) How has your experience of God's forgiveness affected you? How has it shaped your picture of God?

5 Is God's way of relating to us amazing, surprising, hard to believe? Is it possible to lose a sense of wonder at how God has acted toward us? If so, how can we rediscover a sense of wonder at God's way of relating to us?

6 For personal reflection: Do you think God treats your sins more lightly than those of people who are not Christians? Or the opposite? Why?

7 Also for personal reflection: Reread 2:24, which speaks about people getting a bad impression of God from looking at the lives of some who say they believe in him. As people look at you as a Christian, what might they see that would encourage them to believe in Christ? Is there anything that might be an obstacle to observers believing in Christ?

Be sure you understand what another is saying. This is especially true when you disagree with him or her.

Elizabeth W. Flynn and John F. La Faso, *Group Discussion as Learning Process: A Sourcebook*

Approach to Prayer

15 minutes
Use this approach—or create your own!

- ◆ Pray Psalm 14 (quoted in today's reading) and Psalm 6. Pause for silent prayer or for participants to offer short spontaneous prayers. End together with an Our Father.

Saints in the Making

A Moment of Grace

This section is a supplement for individual reading.

God's kindness is meant to lead you to repentance" (Romans 2:4).

"Princess Diana was always a sort of hero of mine," Australian Linda Watson says. "I identified with her—even bought clothes and handbags like hers. I could see the suffering in her eyes, because I had suffered too."

On the day in August 1997 when Diana died in a car crash, Watson was in Perth, Australia, relaxing beside the swimming pool of a friend and fellow brothel owner. "I cried all day," Watson says. "I said, 'God, if Diana with all her beauty and wealth can die, what hope is there for me?' I knew I had hurt so many girls as a madam, by using them as prostitutes. I felt so much pain and shame. I sat by the pool, and I asked God for forgiveness. But I felt so empty. I said, 'God, I need to know what it is like to be a whole person. Get into my life and help me turn this around.'"

Watson describes the next couple of days as a kind of miracle. With a powerful sense of God's help, she sought out an old Bible-quoting friend—Watson used to call her "Looney-Tune Fran"—who would visit her for chats over coffee at her brothel. In short order, Watson was reconciled to God and abandoned the prosperous business she had built up over a period of twenty-four years.

Watson made her transition at the very moment that Western Australia, her home state, was moving toward legalizing prostitution. She immediately got involved in the campaign against the change. This involvement eventually brought her into contact with the Catholic archbishop of Perth, Barry Hickey. Archbishop Hickey had been looking for a way to help women who wanted to get out of prostitution. He suggested to Watson that they work together. The result was the House of Hope. The archdiocese provided a budget and two houses, which Watson has operated as a residential shelter for women trying to leave prostitution and get on with their lives.

Watson's nationwide efforts against legalizing prostitution in Australia and her leadership of the House of Hope have made her a well-known figure in the country. Readers of the Australian *Women's Weekly,* with a readership of three million, chose her as Australia's Most Inspirational Woman of 2003.

RIGHTEOUSNESS HAS ALWAYS BEEN A GIFT

Questions to Begin

15 minutes
Use a question or two to get warmed up for the reading.

1   Name an ancestor or older family member you particularly admire. Do you try to imitate them?

2   Recall a promise that someone made to you when you were growing up. Did they deliver on their promise?

5 minutes
Read the passage aloud. Let individuals take turns reading paragraphs.

The Reading: Romans 3:27–4:25

Misplaced Confidence Is Set Aside

3:27 Then what becomes of boasting? It is excluded. By what law? By that of works? No, but by the law of faith. 28 For we hold that a person is justified by faith apart from works prescribed by the law. 29 Or is God the God of Jews only? Is he not the God of Gentiles also? Yes, of Gentiles also, 30 since God is one; and he will justify the circumcised on the ground of faith and the uncircumcised through that same faith. 31 Do we then overthrow the law by this faith? By no means! On the contrary, we uphold the law.

How Abraham Got Right with God

4:1 What then are we to say was gained by Abraham, our ancestor according to the flesh? 2 For if Abraham was justified by works, he has something to boast about, but not before God. 3 For what does the scripture say? "Abraham believed God, and it was reckoned to him as righteousness." 4 Now to one who works, wages are not reckoned as a gift but as something due. 5 But to one who without works trusts him who justifies the ungodly, such faith is reckoned as righteousness. 6 So also David speaks of the blessedness of those to whom God reckons righteousness apart from works:

> 7 "Blessed are those whose iniquities are forgiven,
>   and whose sins are covered;
> 8 blessed is the one against whom the Lord will not
>   reckon sin."

Abraham: Model for Both Jews and Gentiles

9 Is this blessedness, then, pronounced only on the circumcised, or also on the uncircumcised? We say, "Faith was reckoned to Abraham as righteousness." 10 How then was it reckoned to him? Was it before or after he had been circumcised? It was not after, but before he was circumcised. 11 He received the sign of circumcision as a seal of the righteousness that he had by faith while he was still uncircumcised. The purpose was to make him the ancestor of all who believe without being circumcised and who thus have righteousness

reckoned to them, [12] and likewise the ancestor of the circumcised who are not only circumcised but who also follow the example of the faith that our ancestor Abraham had before he was circumcised.

The Promise to Abraham

[13] For the promise that he would inherit the world did not come to Abraham or to his descendants through the law but through the righteousness of faith. [14] If it is the adherents of the law who are to be the heirs, faith is null and the promise is void. [15] For the law brings wrath; but where there is no law, neither is there violation.

Abraham Believed—and Kept on Believing

[16] For this reason it depends on faith, in order that the promise may rest on grace and be guaranteed to all his descendants, not only to the adherents of the law but also to those who share the faith of Abraham (for he is the father of all of us, [17] as it is written, "I have made you the father of many nations")—in the presence of the God in whom he believed, who gives life to the dead and calls into existence the things that do not exist. [18] Hoping against hope, he believed that he would become "the father of many nations," according to what was said, "So numerous shall your descendants be." [19] He did not weaken in faith when he considered his own body, which was already as good as dead (for he was about a hundred years old), or when he considered the barrenness of Sarah's womb. [20] No distrust made him waver concerning the promise of God, but he grew strong in his faith as he gave glory to God, [21] being fully convinced that God was able to do what he had promised. [22] Therefore his faith "was reckoned to him as righteousness." [23] Now the words, "it was reckoned to him," were written not for his sake alone, [24] but for ours also. It will be reckoned to us who believe in him who raised Jesus our Lord from the dead, [25] who was handed over to death for our trespasses and was raised for our justification.

10 minutes
Choose questions according to your interest and time.

1 Paul uses the word "law" in two
or even three different senses
in 3:27–31. Can you identify the
different meanings?

2 How does 4:7–8 help to explain
what it means to be reckoned
righteous by God?

3 Reread 4:14. Why would God's
promise be "void" if it is to be
inherited by "adherents of the
law"? Does 3:9 help to answer
this question?

4 What does Paul find in Abraham's
faith that makes him a good
model? List as many points as
you can. Give specific verses
to back up your comments.

5 How might the description of
Abraham's faith (4:18–21) apply
to a person's faith in Jesus?
What promises are you "fully
convinced" that God can fulfill?

A Guide to the Reading

If participants have not read this section already, read it aloud. Otherwise go on to "Questions for Application."

3:27–31. Paul has already dealt with two misguided attitudes: feeling morally superior to other people and being complacent in one's relationship with God (2:1–3:20). Here he targets a third, related attitude: the feeling of moral accomplishment ("boasting") that a person may get from following the regulations of the Mosaic law ("works prescribed by the law"). It hardly needs to be said that pride in one's moral excellence is not rooted in Judaism. It is rooted in our flawed human nature and is, in fact, an attitude that tempts all religiously serious people, Christians no less than others.

Paul insists that any sense of achievement on the basis of following the Mosaic law is rendered meaningless by God's action through Christ. Because God is God of all people, not just of Jews, he wished to provide a way of salvation open equally to Jews and gentiles. For this reason, he has provided a way of salvation "apart from works prescribed by the law" (3:28), that is, outside the framework of observing that Mosaic law. This way is Christ. Everyone can attain God's verdict of "justified" by accepting God's righteousness made available in Christ ("by faith"), whether or not they are walking on the path of the Mosaic law (keeping the "works prescribed by the law"). Now that God has opened up this way of salvation outside the framework of Judaism, Paul argues, it is a mistake to focus one's efforts on following the Mosaic law. Where this leaves Judaism is a question that he takes up later in his letter (chapters 9–11).

Some commentators have taken the term "works" in 3:27–28 as a reference to any and all human efforts to obey God. They have interpreted Paul's statement that we are saved by faith in Christ "apart" from works to mean that our human efforts have no value in determining our salvation. At various times, this radical devaluation of human behavior has led to a rejection of the means of cooperating with God's grace, such as sacraments, prayer, fasting, celibacy, the monastic way of life, and so on.

There are two problems with this interpretation. First, Paul is not speaking about all human actions but about obedience to the Mosaic law ("the law" in 3:28 is the Mosaic law, which is binding only on Jews). Second, while Paul believes that our salvation is entirely a gift from God, a matter of God's grace, accessed by faith, from beginning to end (1:17), he does not think that this renders our human cooperation with God's grace unimportant. Rather, he considers our cooperation to be crucial—which is why he spends so much time urging us to cooperate with God (6:12–23; 8; 12). Paul presents us with a paradox—our salvation is *entirely* a gift of God while being also something we are called to "work out" in "fear and trembling" (Philippians 2:12). Paul does not try to explain this paradox—although he does not discourage us from investigating it. However we might try to explain this paradox, it is vitally important to keep both sides in view.

Paul's Jewish conversation partner might well object to the idea of God working outside the framework of the Mosaic law. "The Mosaic law was God's idea in the first place. I can't believe that God would overthrow his own law," the friend might say. "Me neither," Paul replies. "I'm claiming that God's action *outside* the Mosaic law actually *upholds* the law!" (see 3:31; also 3:21). This seemingly contradictory statement calls for some explanation—and Paul proceeds to give it.

4:1–8. Paul makes a simple point: being in a good relationship with God has always rested on the bedrock of God's grace and kindness, accessed through faith rather than on obedience to legal requirements. The illustration Paul offers is Abraham.

It makes sense for Paul to discuss Abraham, because Jews regard him as their ancestor and model. But by focusing on Abraham, Paul has not made things easy for himself. Although Abraham lived before God gave the Mosaic law, Jewish tradition viewed Abraham as an exemplary keeper of God's law and considered Abraham's perfect law keeping as the reason God favored him. One Old Testament writer says of Abraham: "He kept the law of the Most High, and entered into a covenant with him; he certified the covenant in his flesh, and when he was tested he proved faithful. Therefore the Lord assured him with an oath that the nations would be blessed through his offspring; that he would make him as numerous as the dust of the earth . . . and give them an inheritance from sea to sea" (Sirach 44:20–21).

If Abraham related to God primarily in a law-fulfilling manner, and was reckoned righteous for doing so, he would stand as a sign to later Jews that they should seek security with God by keeping the Mosaic law. But, Paul argues, Abraham is not such an example.

Earlier Paul made the easy-to-verify observation that all humans are sinners. Now he applies this observation to Abraham. Abraham, too, was an "ungodly" person (4:5). Paul's Jewish readers might have thought it strange to label Abraham a sinner. But Paul views Abraham as the model convert from paganism, the first man to believe in the one God. If by definition pagans are sinners (see Galatians 2:15), Abraham was a sinner.

And how did ungodly Abraham become righteous, Paul asks? Obviously by faith in God (4:3). Abraham believed in God's ability to set him right—and that is what God did: God "reckoned" Abraham righteous (4:3). God did not reckon Abraham righteous even though he wasn't, in a kind of legal fiction. In 4:7–8, Paul quotes from Psalm 32, a psalm of repentance from sin and divine forgiveness. By linking this psalm with Abraham, Paul suggests that Abraham's faith involved a real change, a turning from sin and an acceptance of God's forgiveness.

4:9–12. It is of great importance that Abraham believed in God and was reckoned righteous *before* being circumcised as a sign of accepting his new relationship with God. In later Israelite tradition, male circumcision became a token of belonging to the Israelite people and committing oneself to fulfill the Mosaic law. The fact that Abraham believed in God (Genesis 15) before being circumcised (Genesis 17) shows that God made him righteous apart from his following the law later given to Moses. Thus Abraham set a precedent for what is happening now: gentiles are receiving God's righteousness by faith in Christ without entering the Israelite covenant and observing the Mosaic law.

4:13–15. Paul argues that our receiving God's life and entering his kingdom *cannot* ultimately be on the basis of fulfilling the Mosaic law.

God promised Abraham a land—the land of Canaan (Genesis 12:1–3; 13:14–16; 17:1–8). In Hebrew, *land* and *earth* are expressed by the same word. This made it possible for Jewish tradition to expand the meaning of the "land" that God promised Abraham to refer to the *earth,* that is, to the whole *world.* Paul now further extends the interpretation of God's words. The promise of the *world* is interpreted as a promise of the *world to come,* that is, the kingdom of God, the new creation, where the human race will enjoy eternal happiness with God (4:13).

Paul reasons that if God planned to give the kingdom, that is, the promise, to "the adherents of the law"(4:14)—those who make keeping the Mosaic law the beginning and end of their relationship with God—his plan would have a fatal flaw. No one obeys the law perfectly. Thus, no one will qualify to receive the promise. As New Testament scholar Christine H. Dodd observed, a promise that will be fulfilled only if an impossible condition is met is really no promise at all.

If God's promise of eternal life is to be made good, Paul concludes, it will have to be on some basis other than fulfillment of the law. This is exactly what God has provided in Jesus Christ. Through Christ, God enables us to inherit the eternal life that he has promised. We will qualify to enter God's kingdom because of the righteousness he gives us, which we take hold of by faith. Thus, God's promise will not be "void."

4:16–25. Receiving God's gift involves an initial act of faith in Christ—and then ongoing faith. We need to keep believing that he is trustworthy and capable of fulfilling his promises. Here, too, Paul points to Abraham as our model. God promised Abraham and Sarah that they would have many descendants through a son who was going to be born to them in their old age (Genesis 17:1–22; 18:1–15). This was implausible, to say the least. At their time of life, Abraham and Sarah had no prospect whatsoever of having a child. Physically, they were as good as dead. But Abraham believed that God would use his creative power to reverse death and give life. Now that God has used his creative power to raise Jesus from the dead, Abraham stands as an encouragement to us to keep on believing that we will share Jesus' conquest of death in the new creation.

As he waited trustingly for a son, Abraham demonstrated that faith is not a single act but an attitude toward God sustained over time (4:17–21). Paul still uses the word *faith,* but its meaning shifts toward what we often call *hope.*

Questions for Application

40 minutes
Choose questions according to your interest and time.

1 What led you to believe in Jesus? What has helped you grow in faith in him? How can you go on growing in faith in him?

2 What experience has impressed on you the fact that your relationship with God is a gift from him? What effect should this realization have on the way you live?

3 Paul refers to God as the One who "justifies the ungodly" (4:5). What difference does this make for how you relate to God?

4 Abraham hoped that God would give him a son (4:18–21). As a Christian, what do you hope God will give you?

5 Paul describes Abraham as "hoping against hope" (4:18). When have you done that? What was the outcome? What did you learn about God and about yourself?

6 When has an experience of forgiveness and reconciliation with another person given you insight into what it means to be forgiven and reconciled to God?

7 In your life, who has been a model of perseverance and hope? What have you learned from this person? How could you imitate them?

8 For personal reflection: What do you boast about—either in Paul's sense of resting your confidence on something or someone or in the sense of tooting your own horn? As far as boasting about yourself, why are the particular things you boast about so important to you? Why is it so important to you for others to notice?

Reading the Bible is not as difficult as many think, but it would be dishonest to say that it is easy.

John L. McKenzie, S.J., *Mastering the Meaning of the Bible*

Approach to Prayer

15 minutes
Use this approach—or create your own!

♦ Sing "Amazing Grace," the hymn
  by John Newton (see the essay
  on page 88).

  Amazing grace! (how sweet the
      sound)
  That saved a wretch like me!
  I once was lost, but now am
      found,
  Was blind, but now I see.

  'Twas grace that taught my heart
      to fear,
  And grace my fears relieved;
  How precious did that grace
      appear
  The hour I first believed!

  Through many danger, toils, and
      snares,
  I have already come;
  'Tis grace has brought me safe
      thus far,
  And grace will lead me home.

  The Lord has promised good to
      me,
  His word my hope secures:
  He will my shield and portion be
  As long as life endures.

  Yes, when this flesh and heart
      shall fail
  And mortal life shall cease,
  I shall possess, within the veil,
  A life of joy and peace.

The earth shall soon dissolve
        like snow,
The sun forbear to shine;
But God, who called me here
        below,
Will be for ever mine.

Another stanza, not written by
John Newton but added later
by an unknown writer, is often
found at the end of the hymn:

When we've been there ten
        thousand years,
Bright shining as the sun,
We've no less days to sing God's
        praise
Than when we first begun.

On Boasting and Baptism

Questions to Begin

15 minutes
Use a question or two to get warmed up for the reading.

1 Describe a situation in which you decided to trust someone. Did your trust turn out to be well-founded?

2 When have you done something deliberately to win another person's trust? Did you succeed?

5 minutes
Read the passage aloud. Let individuals take turns reading
paragraphs.

The Reading: Romans 5:1–11; 6:1–18, 20–23; 7:4–6

Confidence in God's Love

5:1 Therefore, since we are justified by faith, we have peace with God
through our Lord Jesus Christ, 2 through whom we have obtained
access to this grace in which we stand; and we boast in our hope of
sharing the glory of God. 3 And not only that, but we also boast in
our sufferings, knowing that suffering produces endurance, 4 and
endurance produces character, and character produces hope, 5 and
hope does not disappoint us, because God's love has been poured
into our hearts through the Holy Spirit that has been given to us.
6 For while we were still weak, at the right time Christ died
for the ungodly. 7 Indeed, rarely will anyone die for a righteous
person—though perhaps for a good person someone might actually
dare to die. 8 But God proves his love for us in that while we still
were sinners Christ died for us. 9 Much more surely then, now that
we have been justified by his blood, will we be saved through him
from the wrath of God. 10 For if while we were enemies, we were
reconciled to God through the death of his Son, much more surely,
having been reconciled, will we be saved by his life. 11 But more than
that, we even boast in God through our Lord Jesus Christ, through
whom we have now received reconciliation.

Grace: A Misunderstanding

6:1 What then are we to say? Should we continue in sin in order that
grace may abound? 2 By no means! How can we who died to sin
go on living in it? 3 Do you not know that all of us who have been
baptized into Christ Jesus were baptized into his death? 4 Therefore
we have been buried with him by baptism into death, so that, just as
Christ was raised from the dead by the glory of the Father, so we too
might walk in newness of life.
5 For if we have been united with him in a death like his, we
will certainly be united with him in a resurrection like his. 6 We
know that our old self was crucified with him so that the body of sin
might be destroyed, and we might no longer be enslaved to sin. 7 For
whoever has died is freed from sin. 8 But if we have died with Christ,
we believe that we will also live with him. 9 We know that Christ,
being raised from the dead, will never die again; death no longer has

dominion over him. 10 The death he died, he died to sin, once for all; but the life he lives, he lives to God. 11 So you also must consider yourselves dead to sin and alive to God in Christ Jesus.

12 Therefore, do not let sin exercise dominion in your mortal bodies, to make you obey their passions. 13 No longer present your members to sin as instruments of wickedness, but present yourselves to God as those who have been brought from death to life, and present your members to God as instruments of righteousness. 14 For sin will have no dominion over you, since you are not under law but under grace.

No Longer Enslaved by the Power of Sin

15 What then? Should we sin because we are not under law but under grace? By no means! 16 Do you not know that if you present yourselves to anyone as obedient slaves, you are slaves of the one whom you obey, either of sin, which leads to death, or of obedience, which leads to righteousness? 17 But thanks be to God that you, having once been slaves of sin, have become obedient from the heart to the form of teaching to which you were entrusted, 18 and that you, having been set free from sin, have become slaves of righteousness. . . .

20 When you were slaves of sin, you were free in regard to righteousness. 21 So what advantage did you then get from the things of which you now are ashamed? The end of those things is death. 22 But now that you have been freed from sin and enslaved to God, the advantage you get is sanctification. The end is eternal life. 23 For the wages of sin is death, but the free gift of God is eternal life in Christ Jesus our Lord.

The Purpose of Our Freedom

7:4 . . . My friends, you have died to the law through the body of Christ, so that you may belong to another, to him who has been raised from the dead in order that we may bear fruit for God. 5 While we were living in the flesh, our sinful passions, aroused by the law, were at work in our members to bear fruit for death. 6 But now we are discharged from the law, dead to that which held us captive, so that we are slaves not under the old written code but in the new life of the Spirit.

Questions for Careful Reading

4 $\quad$

Romans 5:1–11;
6:1–18, 20–23;
7:4–6

10 minutes
Choose questions according to your interest and time.

1 What might Paul mean when he says that "character produces hope" (5:4)?

2 Verse 5:1 speaks of being "justified." What light does this verse shed on the meaning of justification?

3 Verse 5:9 also speaks about justification. What do verses 5:9–11 tell us about what justification is?

4 What kind of weakness might Paul be talking about in 5:6?

5 In 6:1, Paul raises a question that his readers might well have been wondering about, on the basis of what he said before. What statements in earlier sections of the letter might lead a reader to draw the conclusion that we should "continue in sin in order that grace may abound"?

A Guide to the Reading

*If participants have not read this section already, read it aloud.
Otherwise go on to "Questions for Application."*

5:1–11. Paul cries out in exultation in God's love. Earlier, Paul
criticized boasting about one's moral accomplishments and being
complacent because of one's status in Judaism (2:1, 17–24;
3:27–31). But he is all in favor of boasting when it is a matter of
confidence in God's faithfulness. Paul encourages us to feel secure
in God's mercy and power by fixing our attention on what God has
done and is sure to do for us through Christ. We have the "hope of
sharing the glory of God" (5:2), of recovering our resemblance to
God, becoming living reflectors of his compassion and faithfulness.
The once-unattainable goal (3:23) has come within our reach.

God's love has not removed us from the sinful world or
turned us into supermen and superwomen. We remain vulnerable
and mortal while we wait for the Resurrection. In this condition,
we face the challenge of living out the righteousness that God
has given us, until we come to the final judgment and enter God's
kingdom forever. It is a formidable challenge. But we can be
confident that God will empower us to do our part. Paul assures us
that God will help us get through the sufferings and sorrows of this
world in such a way that we will become more like him (it is *God's*
"character" that we will take on in 5:4). Formerly, we were in the
condition that Paul described in 1:18–3:20, but now God has given
himself to us without limit (5:5). The Spirit within us assures us of
God's love—and gives us a love for God that motivates us to live in
a new way.

Paul's statement in 5:9 is open to a misunderstanding
about God's attitude toward us. Now that we have been justified
by Christ's death, Paul says, we will surely be "saved through him
from the wrath of God." This might seem to raise the specter of
an angry God, whose rage Christ must calm. But Paul is not saying
that God is angry at us. "The wrath" Paul speaks of is not personal
anger in God. This point is clearer in the original Greek, where Paul
has not written "the wrath of God" but simply "the wrath"; the
translators added "of God." This wrath is the terrible doom that
befalls sinners—the deadly consequences of sin. This doom does
not express any desire in God to see us punished; Christ did not

deflect God's anger from us, since God already regarded us with infinite love. This loving God is certain to expend every effort to bring us safely home to himself. Jesus' horrific death on the cross does not reflect the anger of a God who needs to be appeased but the compassion of a God who loves so much that he gave what is most precious to him in order to save us from the consequences of our sins. The Crucifixion is the supreme revelation of the love of both the Son and of the Father.

Being so loved, writes Brendan Byrne, Christians are travelers with their passports stamped "justified" who "can confidently expect that God's love will usher them safely through the final barrier."

6:1–14. Paul has laid an emphasis on God's grace lifting us up, carrying us along, and bearing us home—doing for us what we cannot do for ourselves. Is there, then, anything we need to do? Perhaps we should simply "let go and let God." Indeed, if God loves to save sinners, perhaps we should keep on sinning. Paul says that "where sin increased, grace abounded all the more" (5:20). If the mudflats of sin are where the tide of grace comes flooding in, why don't we just stay right down in the mud? "Good heavens, no!" Paul responds. Grace floods in to lift us *out* of the mud. Once freed, we are supposed to flow along with God's Spirit to better things. Christ has died for us precisely so that we could live in righteousness.

On the cross, Jesus gave himself for us in a twofold manner. He relinquished his life as a sacrifice to God *on our behalf,* and he presented his ultimate obedience to God as an act *in which we may share.* In fact, Jesus invites us to enter into the whole course of his life, death, and resurrection. His experience of life, death, and resurrection is not merely a series of events in the past but a reality that continues to be present in him. When we accept his invitation to faith and baptism, we are plunged into this reality (6:3–10).

Paul speaks of Jesus as a zone, or sphere, of freedom and life. Jesus lived on earth in loving obedience to God's plan for him; united with Jesus, we are enabled to do the same in the circumstances of our lives. Jesus "died to sin" (6:10), rejecting the temptation to sin even to the point of accepting death in obedience to God's plan for him; united to him, we can experience death to selfishness and sin (6:2, 6–7, 11). Jesus rose into a life totally victorious over sin and over the evils that cause human disintegration and death, and he lives now in the glory of God's presence; united to Jesus, we experience his power to overcome sin and live a God-oriented life, and we look forward to sharing in his resurrection (6:5).

Notice the shift in meaning in Paul's discussion of "sin." Earlier, he spoke of sin as wrong *action,* disobedience to God (4:8; 5:16). Here he speaks of sin as a *force* dragging us into wrongdoing (notice how Paul uses terms such as "enslaved," "dominion," and "make you obey"—6:6, 9, 12, 14). Thus, while earlier, Paul spoke of God *forgiving* our sins, he now speaks of God *freeing* us from sin (6:7). Being united with Christ, each of us can proclaim that we no longer belong to sin, our old slave master. That "old slave me," who could not get loose from the power of sin, has been replaced by "me the freedman," "me the freedwoman" (6:6). We still feel the push and pull of sin, but now we also experience a greater power—the power of the Spirit.

Paul expresses the transition into the realm of freedom in Christ as the destruction of "the body of sin" (6:6). Since our bodies do not die when we are baptized, he is obviously not speaking about the body as such. Thus, he is not saying that the body itself is sinful. By "the body of sin," he means the body in a condition of entanglement in sin—which is not the condition God made our bodies to be in.

A key to experiencing freedom in Christ, Paul says, is to "consider" that it is true for us (6:11). Paul does not mean that we should take a mind-over-matter approach, *pretending* that we are not sinners. Recall what happened when God reckoned Abraham righteous: he forgave his sins and put him in a condition of righteousness. God's reckoning involved creating and acknowledging a new *reality* in Abraham (4:1–8). As Christians, we are invited to see and acknowledge the new reality that God has brought about in us through Christ—to believe that Christ really has liberated us from the dominating power of sin.

6:15–23. In this section, Paul compares our justification by Christ to the transfer of a slave from a bad master to a good one. The image serves a purpose, but is somewhat unpleasant. Paul will use a more congenial image further on (8:12–17). Paul's concluding remark here is that if we follow the path of sin, we will get what we deserve, whereas if we follow Jesus, we will get what we do not deserve (6:23).

7:4–6. "You have died to the law," Paul says (7:4). He does not mean that Christians no longer have an obligation to do what is right and avoid doing what is wrong. "God forbid!" Paul would say. "I just finished trying to steer you away from that misunderstanding. Centering your life on Jesus brings righteousness; it doesn't cut you adrift from morality." The Mosaic law, however, is no longer the framework for our relationship with God. That framework left us exposed to the power of sin within ourselves—"our sinful passions"—which we could not bring under control while we were "in the flesh" (7:5). But now that we are in Christ, we will be able to "bear fruit for God" (7:4).

Here Paul uses the term "flesh" in a new way. Previously, he used the word to refer to our physical life (1:3; 4:1). From now on, he uses it to refer to our weakness, mortality, self-centeredness, and tendencies toward sin. But through Christ, God has rescued us from being "in the flesh."

Paul's negative statement about the Mosaic law in 7:6 is simply the latest of a string of such remarks (3:20; 4:15). The question naturally arises whether he thinks there is something inherently wrong with the law. It is time for a clarification, and Paul provides it in the remainder of chapter 7 (see "Our Fractured Selves," page 62).

Questions for Application

40 minutes
Choose questions according to your interest and time.

1 When have you experienced the process that Paul speaks about in 5:3–4? Do things always work the way he says here? What is necessary if suffering is to produce endurance and endurance is to produce character?

2 What helps you to remember the love of God that Paul speaks about in 5:1–11?

3 Where in your life do you most need to exercise hope and resist discouragement? What help do you find in Paul's presentation in 5:1–11?

4 Where would you most wish to grow in being like God? What step could you take toward this goal? What point made in this week's reading could aid your growth?

5 Reread 5:5. How have you experienced the Holy Spirit? What difference does the Spirit make in the process that Paul describes in 5:3–4? What is the role of the Spirit in enabling a person to do what Paul talks about in 6:11–14?

6 Paul speaks of freedom in Christ (6:18, 20). What is Paul's concept of freedom? What are the concepts of freedom that are common in our society today? Which of today's concepts of freedom are compatible with Paul's concept of freedom? Which are not?

7 For personal reflection: Reread 6:1–14. What difference could what Paul speaks about here make in your struggle against sin?

8 For personal reflection: Reread 5:1–11 aloud, then be still for a while in God's presence.

The Bible is the inspired word of God and the book of the Church, but it is also interesting, exciting, maddening, consoling, and instructive. It is above all nourishing.

Gerard S. Sloyan, *So You Mean to Read the Bible: Some Tips for Absolute Beginners*

Approach to Prayer

15 minutes
Use this approach—or create your own!

♦ Ask someone to reread 5:1–11 aloud. Pause for silent reflection and for any prayers that participants may wish to voice. Close with an Our Father.

A Living Tradition

The Old Adam and the New One

This section is a supplement for individual reading.

A t this point in Paul's letter we might ask a question about Jesus' role in saving humanity. Jesus has obviously provided us with a magnificent *example* of obedience to God and self-sacrificing love. But Jesus was just one person. How can his action have an *effect* on all of us?

Paul answers that we humans are not mere individuals; we are joined together, perhaps more deeply than we generally realize. Thus, the sin of our first ancestor, Adam, has had a profound effect on us. Well, Jesus is like Adam: he is the new ancestor of the human race freed from the power of sin. Just as we feel the effects of the disobedience of the first Adam, so we can now feel the effects of the obedience of the second Adam.

This explanation answers one question but raises many others. Theologians have been busy for centuries exploring *how* the effects of Adam's and Christ's actions work their way out in our lives. Paul's point is not to explain how it happens but simply to state that it does (5:19).

In its teaching tradition, the Church has used the term *original sin* to explain what Paul says here about the transmission of sin from Adam to us. The *Catechism of the Catholic Church* tells us:

How did the sin of Adam become the sin of all his descendants? The whole human race is in Adam "as one body of one man." By this "unity of the human race" all men are implicated in Adam's sin, as all are implicated in Christ's justice. Still, the transmission of original sin is a mystery that we cannot fully understand. But we do know by Revelation that Adam had received original holiness and justice not for himself alone, but for all human nature. By yielding to the tempter, Adam and Eve committed a *personal sin,* but this sin affected the *human nature* that they would then transmit *in a fallen state.* It is a sin which will be transmitted by propagation to all mankind, that is, by the transmission of a human nature deprived of original holiness and justice. And that is why original sin is called "sin" only in an analogical sense: it is sin "contracted" and not "committed"—a state and not an act (section 404).

Between Discussions

Our Fractured Selves

In the remainder of chapter 7 (verses 7–25), Paul clarifies some of his earlier negative statements about the Mosaic law. But to understand Paul's clarification, it is necessary to determine what time period he is describing and the identity of the "I" who speaks. To some readers it seems that it is Paul talking about his own life as a Christian. But there is evidence against this view.

Ever since 3:21, Paul has been speaking in terms of "once . . . but now. . . ." He has contrasted the state of people *before* receiving God's grace through Christ and their state *afterward* (especially 6:15–23). His description in 7:7–25 of unsuccessful struggle against sin fits into the "once . . ." side of the contrast, into the picture he has painted of life within the framework of the Mosaic law apart from the grace of Christ (7:4). Paul has been arguing that God's grace in Christ gives us a fundamental freedom from the power of sin. It would hardly support his argument if now he described a person in Christ as a "wretched man . . . captive to the law of sin" (7:24, 23). Further evidence that Paul is speaking here about life *without* Christ, not life *with* Christ, is that he makes no reference to the Holy Spirit.

Against the interpretation that Paul is speaking in an autobiographical way is this: the picture of a wretched man under the thrall of sin does not square with statements he makes about his past life (Galatians 1:13–14; Philippians 3:4–6). Also it is hard to conceive of Paul, a Jew from birth who lived his whole life under the Mosaic law, saying that he "was once alive apart from the law" (7:9).

Rather, it seems, Paul is speaking in a general way about the human struggle against sin apart from God's grace in Christ. In other words, he is describing the condition from which Jesus rescues us. His use of the first-person "I" is a way of making his presentation vivid (compare his use of "you" in 2:17, which has the same purpose).

Some of Paul's description of inner struggle (7:7, citing Exodus 20:17) stretches the limits of plausibility. Surely our desires for other people's possessions do not arise *simply* from being told not to desire them. But Paul does point to a universal experience: being told not to do something often triggers our desire for it.

A father I know forbade his children to watch *The Simpsons* on television because he detested its portrayal of Homer Simpson. It is probably not surprising that some of the children, now grown up, regard the program as one of their favorites. Remember Adam and Eve, for whom the tree of knowledge of good and evil seems to have become peculiarly attractive because God told them to leave it alone (Genesis 2:15–17; 3:1–7). God's instructions about good and evil often provoke a reaction in us—a desire to run our lives independently of him, to decide for ourselves what is good and evil. In any case, by using the good, God-given law of Moses to spur people to wrongdoing, sin shows how deeply evil it is (7:11–13). Here lies Paul's clarification about the Mosaic law: it is good at defining obedience to God but incapable of empowering us to obey.

Sadly, in some form, we continue to experience the inner conflict that Paul describes, even in our lives as Christians. In some part of our makeup we listen to God's instructions and feel conscience-bound to follow them; in another part of ourselves, we close our ears and do what we want. Each of us is locked in conflict with a power of evil within. We rejoice in the goodness of God's commands *and* react against them. Paul underlines our dilemma by stating it three times: 7:14–17, 18–20, 21–23.

Is Paul saying that we are automatons, robots commandeered by evil forces, who no longer have responsibility for our actions (7:14–20)? Actually, he is trying to describe a paradoxical reality: I know what is right, I love it, I will it; yet within this "I" lurks a "Not-I," an "Anti-I," that does not love what is good. There is the well-intentioned "inmost self" me (7:22), and there is the me in which "nothing good dwells" (7:18). Paul's description seems almost in contradiction with itself, yet how else to capture the fracturedness, the lack of integrity we experience in ourselves?

The conflict is unresolvable using our own resources. The Mosaic law—and the law of conscience—express our deepest aspirations. But because we fail to achieve these aspirations, the law stands as a measure of our frustration at the failure to become what we truly want to be. Only God's love in Christ can save us from ourselves.

THE SPIRIT IS LIFE

Questions to Begin

15 minutes
Use a question or two to get warmed up for the reading.

1   What makes you feel frustrated?

2   What did you call your father and mother when you were growing up? What did you call your grandparents?

5 minutes
Read the passage aloud. Let individuals take turns reading paragraphs.

The Reading: Romans 8:1–30

The Spirit Makes Things Happen

8:1 There is therefore now no condemnation for those who are in Christ Jesus. 2 For the law of the Spirit of life in Christ Jesus has set you free from the law of sin and of death. 3 For God has done what the law, weakened by the flesh, could not do: by sending his own Son in the likeness of sinful flesh, and to deal with sin, he condemned sin in the flesh, 4 so that the just requirement of the law might be fulfilled in us, who walk not according to the flesh but according to the Spirit. 5 For those who live according to the flesh set their minds on the things of the flesh, but those who live according to the Spirit set their minds on the things of the Spirit. 6 To set the mind on the flesh is death, but to set the mind on the Spirit is life and peace. 7 For this reason the mind that is set on the flesh is hostile to God; it does not submit to God's law—indeed it cannot, 8 and those who are in the flesh cannot please God.

9 But you are not in the flesh; you are in the Spirit, since the Spirit of God dwells in you. Anyone who does not have the Spirit of Christ does not belong to him. 10 But if Christ is in you, though the body is dead because of sin, the Spirit is life because of righteousness. 11 If the Spirit of him who raised Jesus from the dead dwells in you, he who raised Christ from the dead will give life to your mortal bodies also through his Spirit that dwells in you.

12 So then, brothers and sisters, we are debtors, not to the flesh, to live according to the flesh—13 for if you live according to the flesh, you will die; but if by the Spirit you put to death the deeds of the body, you will live.

14 For all who are led by the Spirit of God are children of God. 15 For you did not receive a spirit of slavery to fall back into fear, but you have received a spirit of adoption. When we cry, "Abba! Father!" 16 it is that very Spirit bearing witness with our spirit that we are children of God, 17 and if children, then heirs, heirs of God and joint heirs with Christ—if, in fact, we suffer with him so that we may also be glorified with him.

Waiting to Be Made New

18 I consider that the sufferings of this present time are not worth comparing with the glory about to be revealed to us. 19 For the creation waits with eager longing for the revealing of the children of God; 20 for the creation was subjected to futility, not of its own will but by the will of the one who subjected it, in hope 21 that the creation itself will be set free from its bondage to decay and will obtain the freedom of the glory of the children of God. 22 We know that the whole creation has been groaning in labor pains until now; 23 and not only the creation, but we ourselves, who have the first fruits of the Spirit, groan inwardly while we wait for adoption, the redemption of our bodies. 24 For in hope we were saved. Now hope that is seen is not hope. For who hopes for what is seen? 25 But if we hope for what we do not see, we wait for it with patience.

Help and Hope

26 Likewise the Spirit helps us in our weakness; for we do not know how to pray as we ought, but that very Spirit intercedes with sighs too deep for words. 27 And God, who searches the heart, knows what is the mind of the Spirit, because the Spirit intercedes for the saints according to the will of God.

28 We know that all things work together for good for those who love God, who are called according to his purpose. 29 For those whom he foreknew he also predestined to be conformed to the image of his Son, in order that he might be the firstborn within a large family. 30 And those whom he predestined he also called; and those whom he called he also justified; and those whom he justified he also glorified.

10 minutes
Choose questions according to your interest and time.

1   According to Paul's statements in this reading, what has God done for us? What is God going to do for us? What specifically is the Holy Spirit doing for us?

2   What are we supposed to do?

3   Based on Paul's statements in this reading, what are signs of the Spirit's presence in us?

4   Does Paul have two entirely separate classes of people in mind in 8:5?

5   Reread what Paul says in 8:19–21 about what will happen to human beings and to the rest of creation when God completes the coming of his kingdom. How do you picture this?

A Guide to the Reading

*If participants have not read this section already, read it aloud.
Otherwise go on to "Questions for Application."*

8:1–11. In a short sentence (8:1), Paul sums up much of what he has been saying. Through Christ, God has brought us out of the dead end of sin and has put us on a new road to himself. Since we could not make ourselves righteous, God has done it for us. He has forgiven our sins and liberated us from the power of sin. We now have the opportunity to live in righteousness by living in Christ, who *is* righteousness. So we can look forward to the future with hope. The certainty of final doom—of being judged guilty at the Last Judgment—has been removed. By God's grace, we can live in a way that will lead us not to final condemnation but to a verdict of "righteous."

In another meaty sentence (8:2), Paul declares the freedom that God has given us. God has set us free from "the law of sin and of death." This fearsome law is not the law of Moses, which is holy (see 7:12). It is the power of sin within us that tries to prevent us from doing God's will (Paul also calls it "another law"—7:23). This power-of-sin law is now replaced by "the law of the Spirit of life in Christ Jesus" (8:2)—which is not a law at all in the sense of a set of regulations, but is the Spirit itself. (Paul would have made it easier for us to follow his meaning if he had stuck to using *law* in just one sense.)

God has "condemned sin" (8:3). Paul does not mean that God showed disapproval of sin—we already knew sin is bad!—but that he defeated it. To get Paul's meaning, we might imagine a courtroom scene: Sin comes into court as the prosecutor; the defendant is the human race. But when Jesus, the representative human being, is found to be sinless, the case against the human race is dropped; the prosecutor is thrown out of court.

By striking down the power of sin and giving us the Holy Spirit, God enables us to fulfill the "just requirement of the law" (8:4). The "law" here and in 8:7 is not the Mosaic law but the requirements of a life pleasing to God (8:8). The basic requirement of a God-pleasing life is, of course, to love (13:8; Galatians 5:14).

If Paul had used an active construction—*we fulfill* the just requirements of the law—he would have put the emphasis on our activity. But by employing a passive construction—"the just requirement of the law might be fulfilled in us"—he puts the accent on God, by whom the law of love is fulfilled in our lives. Thus Paul subtly indicates that our living rightly is God's doing from start to finish, even though it is *our* living. God's Spirit is at work in us, giving us a new mind-set, new desires (8:5). Prompted by the Spirit, we set new goals for ourselves—goals for serving God and other people.

In Paul's view, Christ, living in us by the Spirit, is the key to leading a successful human life. Paul would have agreed with the Supremes' old song that reminded us love doesn't come easy. In fact, love is difficult. As soon as we set out to do it, we experience inner resistance, we feel the weight of our selfishness. In earthly life, we never escape human frailty; our bodies are destined to die (8:10). But into our weakness, Christ has come. We can be confident, then, that God, who raised his righteous Son from the dead, will also raise our "mortal bodies" because of the righteousness that he has placed in us and will maintain in us by his Spirit (8:10–11).

8:12–13. Ever the realist, Paul never loses sight of the moral conflict that continues in our lives after we put our faith in Christ. In fact, Paul views the Christian life as an ongoing struggle. It requires determination and effort to "put to death the deeds of the body" (8:13). We can do it only "by the Spirit" (8:13). Living well is a matter of being "led by the Spirit" (8:14). While it requires great resolution on our part, and great exertions, to grasp the freedom that God has given us in Christ, the initiative always lies with the Spirit. No matter how hard we must work, our part is always fundamentally a matter of cooperating with the Spirit who lives within us. In another letter, Paul declares that our very desire and willingness to accept God's help are God's gifts to us (Philippians 2:13).

Do we find at times that our struggle against sin looks more like Paul's description of the Spirit-less pre-Christian life in chapter 7 than the Spirit-filled Christian life in chapter 8? If so, perhaps we should reexamine our relationship with the Holy Spirit.

Are we seeking the help of the Spirit? Are we cooperating with his initiatives in our lives?

8:14–17. Earlier, Paul said that Christ has freed us from enslavement to sin and has made us "slaves of righteousness" (6:18). Now he uses a more appealing—and more profound—image: our transition into a new relationship with God is like adoption. Christians in Paul's day, unlike their Jewish and pagan neighbors, were in the habit of addressing God as *Father.* They even used the Aramaic word that Jesus, an Aramaic-speaker, used in his prayer: *Abba. Abba* can be translated "Father" or, more familiarly, "Dad." "Daddy," which is a word used by little children, is not the best rendering, because the Aramaic word was used not only by small children but also by adults in addressing their fathers—although, for Americans in the South who call their father "Daddy" even as adults, it would be a perfectly accurate translation.

As sons and daughters of God, we are his "heirs" (8:17). St. Thomas Aquinas remarked that the wealth of God is God himself, so if we are heirs of God, it is God himself whom we hope to inherit. This hope is the framework in which Paul urges us to view all our sufferings.

8:18–25. Paul directs our attention beyond ourselves to glimpse the larger picture of God's plans. Look at the universe, he says. The universe was given to us as the means by which we could serve and glorify God. It was supposed to attain lasting satisfaction in us, the human race, as we step into God's eternal kingdom. If we fail to find lasting fulfillment in God, the universe cannot achieve lasting satisfaction either; it just goes on and on—or "round and round," as the author of Ecclesiastes observed (Ecclesiastes 1:1–11). Our turning away from God into sin has frustrated the purpose of creation; at present, it is in a bondage to "futility" (8:20). But now it looks forward to satisfying its purpose and attaining lasting satisfaction when the human race enters into the glory of God's kingdom through Christ.

When did creation fall into this condition? How does Paul's view of the universe fit with the understanding known to science?

What will it mean for the universe to be freed from futility? Similar questions arose earlier regarding the when and how of humanity's enslavement to sin. As there, here also Paul leaves many questions unanswered.

Paul has now pointed to two signs of the Spirit's presence within us. First, there is our trust in God's fatherly love (8:15–17). Second—and this is perhaps surprising—there is our dissatisfaction with the present world, our sorrow at the condition of the world and ourselves (8:23). Paul views this restlessness as a sign that the Spirit is stirring us with a longing for the better world to come—the world in which everything, including ourselves, will reflect God's goodness and "glory" (8:18). Compare Jesus' equally surprising statements that those who "mourn" and "hunger and thirst for righteousness" are "blessed" (Matthew 5:4, 6).

8:26–27. Also, perhaps surprisingly, the great apostle Paul is familiar with the inability to know how to pray or what to pray for. Prayer may begin with a bold and trusting "Father!" but then trail off into inarticulate groaning. Never mind, Paul says. God counts our inarticulate longing as prayer. In this weakness, too, the Spirit is present. The Spirit will pray within us, even when we cannot find the words to express the jumble of awe, sorrow, and joy that we experience in the presence of God.

8:28–30. Finally, Paul reminds us of God's sovereignty. We have life with God because God freely loves, decides ahead of time, calls, justifies, transforms. This sovereign God is able to accomplish good, even in the most grievous suffering and most calamitous losses. Again, Paul's wording is subtly significant: he first speaks of us as "those who love God" but then shifts the accent from us to God by referring to us as those "who are called according to his purpose" (8:28). We love God only because God has created us and has placed his love within us (5:5). At the end of time, Paul promises us, we will see—the entire creation will see—all that God has done for us through his Son.

Questions for Application

40 minutes
Choose questions according to your interest and time.

1 Reread 8:5. How would you explain Paul's meaning? What do you set your mind on?

2 What does it mean to be "led by the Spirit" (8:14)? What does the Spirit lead a person to do? How can a person grow in knowing where the Spirit is leading? What does Paul say in this reading that might help to answer this question?

3 Reread 8:15. Do you call God *Father* when you pray? Do you think of God as your Father? Do you have difficulty thinking of God as Father? How could you open yourself more to God's fatherly love for you?

4 What does it mean to suffer with Christ (8:17)? Can any kind of suffering be suffered with Christ? What element makes our suffering a suffering with Christ? What difference does it make whether one's suffering is with Christ?

5 When have you especially experienced the kind of inner groaning that Paul speaks about in 8:23? Do you express your sorrows and frustrations to God? How does he respond?

6 When do you find it difficult to pray? What encouragement do you find in 8:26–27? What aids does the Spirit use to help you to pray?

7 When have you seen the truth of Paul's statement in 8:28? Is this truth always demonstrated in earthly life?

8 For personal reflection: Do you often feel guilty? Is it because you have actually done something wrong or for other reasons? Do you need to ask God's forgiveness for something? someone else's forgiveness, also? What part should the sacrament of Reconciliation have in this process?

A prayerful reading of the New Testament should normally leave us with a sense of wonder.

Eugene LaVerdiere, S.S.S., *The New Testament in the Life of the Church: Evangelization, Prayer, Catechetics, Homiletics*

Approach to Prayer

15 minutes
Use this approach—or create your own!

♦ Pray together this prayer of hope by Venerable Charles de Foucauld. Pause for silent reflection. End together with an Our Father.

My God, speak to me of hope. . . .

You forbid me ever to become discouraged at the sight of my shortcomings or to tell myself: "I can't go any further. The road to heaven is too narrow. . . ."

You forbid me to look at the infinite graces you have showered on me and at the unworthiness of my present life and to tell myself: "I haven't made good use of so many graces. I should be a saint, and I'm a sinner. After all God has done, there's nothing good in me. I'll never get to heaven." You want me to hope in spite of everything.

Heaven and me, this perfection and my wretched state—whatever can these things have in common? Your heart, my Lord Jesus. Your heart creates the link between two things that are so unlike.

This section is a supplement for individual reading.

Some scholars have identified the prayer of the Spirit that Paul describes in Romans 8:26–27 with the mysterious praying "in a tongue" that he discusses in 1 Corinthians 14. One who makes this connection is New Testament scholar George T. Montague, S.M. Montague also believes the gift of "tongues" is a gift given by the Spirit today.

My self is a totality, and part of the anguish of human existence is to find how limited are my channels of self-expression when I want to *totally* communicate, or when I want to express even partially some inward mystery of my self. I go to the funeral parlor to visit a close friend whose dearest one has died, and "words cannot express" what I want to say. At other times my joy is so great that I feel like only an explosion can release it. At other times I am troubled or depressed without knowing fully why—my "spirit" in all these cases looks for some way to process what it is experiencing, to "get it out." And rational speech just will not do. . . .

But the New Testament . . . speaks of a special gift of prayer by which man's spirit may be activated with a language of the spirit, enabling depth to speak unto depth (1 Corinthians 14:2, 14). It is not primarily a gift of communicating in a foreign language. . . . Rather, the gift is primarily non-rational prayer (. . . 1 Corinthians 14:2). . . .

But *what* is it saying? The very question reveals perhaps the insatiable desire to comprehend and control the language, whereas Paul in Romans 8:26–27 sees the transcending of this control as the specific advantage of the language of the Spirit. . . .

"Why does the hummingbird hum?" begins an old joke. "Because he doesn't know the words." With childlike seriousness we might ask, why does the Spirit-filled Christian pray in tongues? Because he doesn't know the words—and because, furthermore, he knows the Father doesn't care, for the Father is not impressed with rhetoric but only with the language of the heart. And if the heart is speaking by the power of the Holy Spirit, then the one praying is sharing in the eternal mutual utterance of the Father and Son.

From *Riding the Wind: Learning the Ways of the Spirit*

GROUNDS FOR HOPE—
AND LOVE

Questions to Begin

15 minutes
Use a question or two to get warmed up for the reading.

1 Who has been on your side in a situation of conflict or trouble?

2 When was the last time someone did something for you or gave something to you cheerfully?

Read the passage aloud. Let individuals take turns reading
paragraphs.

The Reading: Romans 8:31–39; 12; 13:8–10

God's Unbreakable Commitment

8:31 What then are we to say about these things? If God is for us,
who is against us? 32 He who did not withhold his own Son,
but gave him up for all of us, will he not with him also give us
everything else? 33 Who will bring any charge against God's elect?
It is God who justifies. 34 Who is to condemn? It is Christ Jesus,
who died, yes, who was raised, who is at the right hand of God,
who indeed intercedes for us. 35 Who will separate us from the love
of Christ? Will hardship, or distress, or persecution, or famine, or
nakedness, or peril, or sword? 36 As it is written,
  "For your sake we are being killed all day long;
    we are accounted as sheep to be slaughtered."
37 No, in all these things we are more than conquerors through him
who loved us. 38 For I am convinced that neither death, nor life,
nor angels, nor rulers, nor things present, nor things to come, nor
powers, 39 nor height, nor depth, nor anything else in all creation,
will be able to separate us from the love of God in Christ Jesus our
Lord.

The Life That God Makes Possible

12:1 I appeal to you therefore, brothers and sisters, by the mercies of
God, to present your bodies as a living sacrifice, holy and acceptable
to God, which is your spiritual worship. 2 Do not be conformed to
this world, but be transformed by the renewing of your minds, so
that you may discern what is the will of God—what is good and
acceptable and perfect.
      3 For by the grace given to me I say to everyone among
you not to think of yourself more highly than you ought to think,
but to think with sober judgment, each according to the measure
of faith that God has assigned. 4 For as in one body we have many
members, and not all the members have the same function, 5 so
we, who are many, are one body in Christ, and individually we are
members one of another. 6 We have gifts that differ according to the
grace given to us: prophecy, in proportion to faith; 7 ministry, in

ministering; the teacher, in teaching; 8 the exhorter, in exhortation; the giver, in generosity; the leader, in diligence; the compassionate, in cheerfulness.

9 Let love be genuine; hate what is evil, hold fast to what is good; 10 love one another with mutual affection; outdo one another in showing honor. 11 Do not lag in zeal, be ardent in spirit, serve the Lord. 12 Rejoice in hope, be patient in suffering, persevere in prayer. 13 Contribute to the needs of the saints; extend hospitality to strangers.

14 Bless those who persecute you; bless and do not curse them. 15 Rejoice with those who rejoice, weep with those who weep. 16 Live in harmony with one another; do not be haughty, but associate with the lowly; do not claim to be wiser than you are. 17 Do not repay anyone evil for evil, but take thought for what is noble in the sight of all. 18 If it is possible, so far as it depends on you, live peaceably with all. 19 Beloved, never avenge yourselves, but leave room for the wrath of God; for it is written, "Vengeance is mine, I will repay, says the Lord." 20 No, "if your enemies are hungry, feed them; if they are thirsty, give them something to drink; for by doing this you will heap burning coals on their heads." 21 Do not be overcome by evil, but overcome evil with good.

The Last Word: Love!

13:8 Owe no one anything, except to love one another; for the one who loves another has fulfilled the law. 9 The commandments, "You shall not commit adultery; You shall not murder; You shall not steal; You shall not covet"; and any other commandment, are summed up in this word, "Love your neighbor as yourself." 10 Love does no wrong to a neighbor; therefore, love is the fulfilling of the law.

10 minutes
Choose questions according to your interest and time.

1 What does Paul mean by "this world" (12:2)? What statements in chapters 2 and 3 help explain what he means?

2 What does Paul mean when he says, "Let love be genuine" (12:9)?

3 What does it mean to "rejoice in hope" (12:12)? How does rejoicing in hope go along with being "patient in suffering" (also 12:12)? What does rejoicing in hope mean in the kinds of situations Paul mentions in 8:35–36? How does rejoicing in hope go along with weeping "with those who weep" (12:15)? Does it mean saying, "Cheer up"?

4 When have you seen an example of 12:21 in action?

A Guide to the Reading

If participants have not read this section already, read it aloud. Otherwise go on to "Questions for Application."

Where has Paul's lengthy explanation of sin and grace brought us? Still bogged down in our sins? Clearly not. With a free pass to heaven, no matter how we live? Not that, either. By faith in Christ, we have received forgiveness and reconciliation with God; we have been incorporated into Christ's life, death, and resurrection; we have been filled with the power of the Spirit. God has given us his own righteousness, and in his righteousness he will bring us home. Bogged down we are not. Yet we must play our part, holding on to God's gift of righteousness and living it out (see 8:4). Certainly the ability to keep hold of it—indeed, even the desire to do so—is a gift continuously given us by the Spirit. Nevertheless, our response to God's action, however modest, is crucial. So Paul now encourages us to persevere, hopeful about the outcome of our lives.

8:31–39. We have every reason for hope, Paul proclaims, for God is on our side. He was already on our side when we were alienated from him by our sins (5:8). Now, with his Son interceding for us in heaven (8:34) and his Spirit interceding for us from within our hearts (8:26–27), *nothing* can separate us from his love. There is no denying that our part in cooperating with God may be arduous. Obedience may involve suffering, even death. But our death, whenever and however it comes, is foreseen by God and included in his plans for us. Distress and persecution are powerless to wrench us out of the hands of the sovereign God. Indeed, in his hands, troubles and opposition can even play a constructive role in shaping us into the men and women God wishes us to be—men and women who resemble him.

Very well, we are called to live out the righteousness that God has given us in Christ. What does such a life look like? How does it work? In the next section, Paul offers some basic principles.

12:1–2. Since we have become united to Jesus through faith and baptism (see especially 6:4–11), we should enter into his relationship with the Father. As Jesus offered his whole life obediently to the Father (5:19), so should we.

Paul makes his appeal "by the mercies of God" (12:1). This is not empty rhetoric. It is a reminder, New Testament scholar Joseph Fitzmyer, S.J., writes, that "it is by God's mercy that this new

Christian life is lived. It is not we who bring it about that the gospel transforms our lives, but God's mercy that transforms our lives."

We live out our offering of self to God in the ordinary circumstances of our lives. Our self-offering is something we do not only in church but outside of church. Thus our work, recreation, shopping, and whatever else we do becomes worship—"spiritual worship" (12:1)—if we offer it to God and live it in the Spirit. True worship is to return our lives to God in thanks. To live this way is to worship God. By living in a way that pleases God, with faith in Christ and trust in God's love, we bear witness to others that God is loving and trustworthy. In this way, our lives become an expression of praise to God for his goodness.

Furthermore, Paul says, since you entered into Jesus' death, die to the kind of thinking that is centered on self and on this present world. Raised up with Jesus, take on a new way of looking at life, in which God's love lies at the center of attention. "Do not be conformed to this world" (12:2; see 8:5–6; 1 Corinthians 7:31). Be conformed to the world—or age—to come, for it has already dawned in Christ (13:11–14), and you already belong to it.

Paul wants us to "discern what is the will of God—what is good and acceptable and perfect" (12:2). During an earlier period of his life, Paul's approach to discovering God's will was to study the Mosaic law and determine its requirements for each situation. Now he has a new approach: to seek God's will anew in each moment by looking for opportunities to use the gifts the Spirit gives (12:3–8) and looking for opportunities to love (12:9–21). Right and wrong have not changed; the moral law has not become unimportant. But Paul's focus has shifted from keeping his eye on the Mosaic law to keeping his eye on the Spirit.

12:3–8. Paul has called us to have a new mentality—to consider ourselves "dead to sin and alive to God in Christ" (6:11). This change in our thinking doesn't happen as we just sit and think about it, or even simply as we pray; it happens as we use the gifts God gives us for the service of other people. As we express love, compassion, humility, and kindness, selfish ways of thinking become dislodged, and we begin to see all of life in its relationship to the creator.

Significantly, Paul launches his appeal to use our gifts with a reminder to exercise humble realism about ourselves (12:3). But why does he urge us to evaluate ourselves according to the measure of our *faith* rather than according to the *gifts* we have received? The reason, perhaps, is that faith, which is itself a gift from God, is our God-given capacity to respond to his graces and use his gifts. Faith is openness to God's presence and action. The "measure of faith that God has assigned" (12:3) to each of us is our particular receptivity to him. We should each serve God according to the receptivity, the faith, he has given us. If ours seems small compared to that of others, there is no cause to worry. We should just use what we have. Even if our faith is as tiny as a little seed, God can make great use of it (Matthew 17:20).

Some of the gifts Paul mentions (12:6–8) have broader significance than the translation suggests. The term rendered "ministry" (12:7) simply means serving, acting as an agent—a role we are all called to play in some fashion, as we serve the people in our lives and act as the agent of God's love to them. The Greek word translated "leader" (12:8) also means "protector." Paul may be thinking of Christians whose wealth and social standing put them in a position to look out for poorer members. Our society is much different from that of the Romans, but this is a role that, in some fashion, many of us can play today.

12:9–13. Commenting on this section, Thomas Aquinas observes that after discussing particular gifts, Paul now speaks about the gift given to everyone: charity. Earlier in the letter, Paul spoke often of love—God's love, that is (5:5, 8; 8:35, 39). Only now, having made it clear that God has loved us first, does Paul speak about our responsibility to love. Paul assumes that human love is possible only as a response to the divine love.

♦ Let your love be genuine, Paul urges. Let your love be from the heart, since the Holy Spirit is in your hearts, giving you God's love (5:5).

♦ Paul prods us to action. Don't "lag" (12:11): don't be hesitant, don't give in to weariness, sloth, or timidity. We can get ourselves moving, with God's help. But what about being—

♦ "ardent in spirit" (12:11): can we make ourselves fervent and eager? Possibly, Paul is referring here to the Holy Spirit. His message could be paraphrased: "Be aglow with the Spirit. Let the Spirit bubble up within you."

♦ "Persevere in prayer" (12:12). Having spoken about hardships and suffering, Paul knows from his own experience the importance of looking to God for help (recall 8:15–16, 26–27).

12:14–21. Paul thinks it is especially important to take a constructive approach to misunderstanding and hostility. His reference to God's wrath, as we have seen earlier, does not mean God's personal anger at sinners but the doom that befalls them. God's "vengeance" is not a mean-spirited infliction of pain but an exercise of his supreme authority to bring justice. Paul's advice in 12:19–20 is difficult to interpret. Some have thought him to mean that we should simply leave punishment of others' sins to God, or even that we should intensify their punishment by making their hostility to us less defensible. Such negative interpretations seem unlikely, however, in light of Paul's charitable activism: "Bless those who persecute you. . . . Overcome evil with good" (12:14, 21). Possibly heaping burning coals on someone's head is a vivid figurative way of saying, "Stimulate people to change their thinking by doing good to them."

13:8–10. Finally, Paul tells us what he regards as the core of the Mosaic law, the inner principle of enduring value. If you understand the law rightly, he says, you will see that essentially it is all about love. Love is God's purpose for our lives. Thus we should approach each situation in our lives not by asking, "What precept of the law applies here?" but by asking, "How can I love?" This is not an easy way to live!

Questions for Application

40 minutes
Choose questions according to your interest and time.

1   Reread 8:35. When have you experienced what Paul is talking about here? What effect will it have on how you live today?

2   Reread 8:35–39. If you were to make up your own list of things that cannot separate you from God, what would you put on the list?

3   Read Mark 15:33–34. Are there differences between the scene at the cross and what Paul says in 8:35–39? How do you see the relationship between these two passages?

4   Identify an area in which you have grown in love. What is one lesson you have learned? How could you apply that lesson today?

5 Pick one point in 12:1–21 that
has special meaning for you.
Why is it important for you?
What will you do in response?

6 Pick another point in 12:1–21,
and identify someone who has
been a good example of doing
what Paul speaks of. How could
you imitate this person?

**Just as the body dies if it does not receive physical food, so the
soul dies if it does not receive spiritual food. Why do I say this?
Because some people are accustomed to say, "I have no need for
sacred Scripture; reverence for God is enough for me." Therefore, I
have said, "Just as there are foods for the body, so also the sacred
Scriptures are the foods for the soul."**

St. Jerome, Commentary on Psalm 127

Approach to Prayer

15 minutes
Use this approach—or create your own!

◆ Reread Romans 12:1–2. Then pray together this prayer by St. Pio of Pietrelcina.

Stay with me, Lord, because I
am weak and I need Your
strength, that I may not
fall so often. . . .
Stay with me, Lord, for You are
my light and without You I
am in darkness.
Stay with me, Lord, to show me
Your will. . . .
Stay with me, Lord, if You
wish me to be faithful to
You. . . .
Let me recognize You as
Your disciples did at the
breaking of the bread,
so that the Eucharistic
Communion be the Light
which disperses the
darkness, the force which
sustains me, the unique joy
of my heart.
Stay with me, Lord, because at
the hour of my death, I
want to remain united to
You. . . .
Stay with me, Lord, for it is You
alone I look for, Your
Love, Your Grace,
Your Will, Your Heart,
Your Spirit, because I
love You and ask no other
reward but to love you
more and more. . . . Amen.

Saints in the Making

A Rather Ordinary Saint

6 *Romans 8:31–39;*
12; 13:8–10

This section is a supplement for individual reading.

Gianna Beretta Molla: hardworking physician, deeply-in-love wife, sometimes-stressed-out mother, skiing and opera enthusiast. Are there the makings of sainthood here?

Gianna Molla attracted public attention in Milan, Italy, in 1962, shortly after giving birth to her fourth child. A uterine tumor had been discovered during the pregnancy. She rejected a surgical solution that would end the pregnancy and chose a minimal procedure to preserve the baby's life, knowing that this put her own life at risk. The baby girl was born healthy at term. Gianna died a few days later.

Perhaps because the right to life of unborn children has been such a point of contention in recent years, someone suggested that Gianna be considered a saint. Despite the heroic nature of her decision, however, the canonization idea would not have gone anywhere, except that when church authorities looked into her life, they found that this pediatrician, family woman, and lover of things beautiful had, indeed, lived a very holy life. Her fateful decision was simply an expression of the whole way she lived—caring deeply for other people, trusting God, hoping for the best (Gianna hoped she would survive the pregnancy), and putting others' needs ahead of her own.

In chapter 12 of his letter to the Romans, St. Paul sketches a lifestyle that is both ordinary and extraordinary: seek God's will, use your gifts for other people, let love be genuine. This way of life demands total commitment but doesn't necessarily involve an unusual vocation. If God calls you to an ordinary life, Paul seems to say, live it with extraordinary love.

An ordinary vocation is often the way to sainthood, although it is not generally the way to *canonized* sainthood. If Gianna Molla had not risked her life for her child and lost, it is unlikely that she would be St. Gianna today (she was canonized in 2004, with her husband and children in attendance). Yet her canonization draws our attention to her whole life—and what we find there is nothing out of the ordinary, except in the sense that she was determined to find God's will in each moment and, to the best of her ability, to serve the people in her life. In that way, she is a model for us all. To learn more about her, see "Resources," page 96.

87

Truly Amazing Grace

Perhaps the most amazing thing about the well-loved hymn "Amazing Grace" is that *after* the "hour" the author "first believed," he worked for several years in the African slave trade.

John Newton went to sea in 1736 at the age of eleven. He later wrote that by the time he turned twenty, "no vice was too wretched or mean for me." In 1748, in the North Atlantic, a massive storm almost destroyed the ship on which he served. As death seemed imminent, Newton cried out to God. When the shattered vessel finally limped into port, Newton felt that he had been "snatched, by a miracle, from sinking into the ocean and into hell."

The experience frightened Newton into a better life, but not into a relationship with God. Looking back, he wrote, "I consider this as the beginning of my return to God, or rather of his return to me; but I cannot consider myself to have been a believer (in the full sense of the word) till a considerable time afterwards." For a few months, he slid back into his old sins, but then, gradually, became more serious about his faith. It was during this period of growing religious interest, between 1749 and 1754, that Newton worked in the slave trade—without a qualm of conscience.

As first officer on a slave-transport ship, Newton wrote to a friend in England, "I assure you I never was so happy in my life." At the same time he wrote, "I trust, I have been delivered from the power and dominion of sin . . . his powerful grace has hitherto preserved me . . . he will be my guide and guard to the end."

On slave ships, kidnapped Africans were chained side by side in the sweltering, stinking hold for weeks. Wallowing in vomit and excrement, many died en route. After one ship on which he served unloaded its human cargo in Charleston, South Carolina, Newton attended church services in the city and went into the woods for solitary prayer. "I began to taste the sweets of communion with God in the exercise of prayer and praise," he wrote. "I had, for the most part, peace of conscience, and my strongest desires were toward the things of God."

Soon, Newton became the captain of a slave ship. He embarked on his voyages with confidence in God's help. In his journal he noted, "When I consider that in the most inhospitable climate and the most distressed circumstances I shall be

88

surrounded with a Providence always able, always ready, to supply my every deficiency. . . . I then grow composed and ready to undertake whatever is necessary with cheerfulness." On one voyage, he wrote a biblical quotation at the beginning of the ship's log: "They that go down to the sea in ships, that do business in great waters; these see the works of the Lord, and his wonders in the deep" (Psalm 107:23–24, King James Version).

Years later, Newton wrote: "During the time I was engaged in the slave trade, I never had the least scruple as to its lawfulness. I was, upon the whole, satisfied with it, as the appointment Providence had marked out for me."

As captain, Newton delegated most of the work. Especially when the ship was at sea, his responsibilities demanded little of his time, and he devoted himself to long hours of prayer, Scripture reading, and study. On Sundays he led a prayer service on deck with the crew. His biographer William E. Phipps writes: "When Newton was a slave-ship captain, profanity seems to have headed his list of the seven deadly sins, the others being Sabbath breaking, gambling, wenching, boozing, dancing, and theatergoing." Kidnapping human beings, taking them thousands of miles from their homes, and forcing them into grueling, lifelong, unpaid labor were not on Newton's list of sins.

After several voyages, Newton took a job as a customs official in Liverpool, England. Here, he continued his studies and began to do some preaching as a layman in churches. He became friends with John Wesley, the great English preacher and founder of the Methodist movement. Wesley was one of the few men of his day in England to take a public stand against slavery. Apparently through Wesley's influence, Newton's thinking began to change. He came to regard slavery with disgust.

In 1764, Newton was ordained as a priest in the Church of England and took a small, rural pastorate. Over the next sixteen years, he became an exemplary pastor—attentive to the needs of poor residents, energetic in reaching out to young people, and determined to preach and teach in ways that ordinary people could understand. He opposed religious intolerance and criticized Protestants who sought to restrict Catholics' religious liberty. To encourage and uplift his congregation, Newton wrote hymns. One was the hymn now called "Amazing Grace."

After 1780, when he moved to a church in downtown London, Newton's opposition to slavery shifted from private criticism to public confrontation. He urged a young member of Parliament named William Wilberforce, who sought his advice, to advocate the abolition of slavery. In 1788, Newton published one of the first books to expose the slave trade for what it was. *Thoughts upon the African Slave Trade* described the routine degradation, torture, and rape in the slave trade. Since Newton spoke with the authority of direct experience, the book made a deep impression on English popular opinion.

In his hymn, Newton spoke of "the hour" of believing. But from his own experience, he knew that a single experience of God's grace, however sudden and powerful, could only be one step in a process of coming to know God, understand his will, and follow his ways. His own conversion in the storm, when God saved him from death and hell, "made the first impression upon my heart," he later wrote. But "the eyes of my mind were not opened until long afterwards." Only much later did he come to see how terribly blind he remained after the "hour" that marked the beginning of his conversion. Of the slave trading that followed his initial conversion, "my heart now shudders," he wrote in *Thoughts upon the African Slave Trade.* "I am bound in conscience to take shame to myself by a public confession, which, however sincere, comes too late to prevent or repair the misery and mischief to which I have, formerly, been accessory."

If God's grace seemed "sweet" to Newton when his ship survived the storm in 1748, it must have seemed more precious twenty-five years later, when he realized how patient God had been with him through all the sin that followed. His earlier gratitude for being rescued from death must have matured into gratitude for being forgiven for doing things he later came to detest.

Newton's experience points us away from thinking that any spiritual experience of God's love, no matter how genuine, can totally transform us. Growth in the Christian life, whether for Francis of Assisi or for Joe and Becky Churchgoer, occurs over time, as we respond to God's grace. "The Christian's growth is not instantaneous,"

Newton wrote, "but by degrees, as the early dawn increases in bright-ness till the perfect day. . . . In this manner your views of gospel truth shall increase in clarity. . . . A Christian is not a hasty growth, like a mushroom, but rather like the oak, the progress of which is hardly perceptible, but in time becomes a great deep-rooted tree."

Newton's postconversion blindness stands as a warning to us. A person who has real spiritual experiences and shows signs of serious response to God's grace may, nevertheless, be dangerously blind to the effects of his or her actions on other people. Looking at Newton, I must confront the possibility that in years to come I may look back and see for the first time the adverse effects of my actions on people around me—my wife, my children, the people I work with, my neighbors in city, nation, and world.

God's grace in John Newton's life causes me amazement and also discomfort, even protest. It is easy to welcome a God gracious enough to bring an out-of-control young sailor to his senses and forgive his blasphemies and immoral lifestyle. It is not so easy to applaud a God who sticks with that same sailor through a period of terrible moral blindness. Newton committed the kinds of foul injustices that, in a just world, would bring the most severe penalties. It takes only a moment to look at things from the point of view of Newton's victims to see that, from a human point of view, his behavior was almost impossible to forgive, no matter how repentant he might ever have felt about it. Yet the gradual change in Newton's life and thinking reflects the grace of a God who patiently led him to see the evil of his ways, to reject it, and finally to oppose it. God brought Newton to see the truth, rather than pitch him overboard in righteous indignation. Appalling grace! The split-level picture of Newton meditating with pleasure on his Bible in the captain's cabin, while men and women lie belowdecks, chained in their own filth, is humanly unendurable. Presumably, it was divinely unendurable, also: if any situation ever cried to heaven for justice, this did. Yet God's righteousness is of such a kind that he was not willing to give up, even on John Newton.

This God seems too kind to the sinner, too patient with the morally obtuse. Yet some of us, at least, knowing what we know about ourselves, may whisper, "Not *too* kind."

91

Suggestions for Bible Discussion Groups

L ike a camping trip, a Bible discussion group works best if you agree on where you're going and how you intend to get there. Many groups use their first meeting to talk over such questions and reach a consensus. Here is a checklist of issues, with bits of advice from people who have experience in Bible discussions. (A planning discussion will go more smoothly if the leaders have thought through the following issues beforehand.)

Agree on your purpose. Are you getting together to gain wisdom and direction for your lives? to finally get acquainted with the Bible? to support one another in following Christ? to encourage those who are exploring—or reexploring—the Church? for other reasons?

Agree on attitudes. For example: "We're all beginners here." "We're here to help one another understand and respond to God's word." "We're not here to offer counseling or direction to one another." "We want to read Scripture prayerfully." What do *you* wish to emphasize? Make it explicit!

Agree on ground rules. Barbara J. Fleischer, in her useful book *Facilitating for Growth,* recommends that a group clearly state its approach to the following:

- ◆ *Preparation.* Do we agree to read the material and prepare answers to the questions before each meeting?
- ◆ *Attendance.* What kind of priority will we give to our meetings?
- ◆ *Self-revelation.* Are we willing to help the others in the group gradually get to know us—our weaknesses as well as our strengths, our needs as well as our gifts?
- ◆ *Listening.* Will we commit ourselves to listening to one another?
- ◆ *Confidentiality.* Will we keep everything that is shared *with* the group *in* the group?
- ◆ *Discretion.* Will we refrain from sharing about the faults and sins of people who are not in the group?
- ◆ *Encouragement and support.* Will we give as well as receive?
- ◆ *Participation.* Will we give each person the time and opportunity to make a contribution?

Groups

You could probably take a pen and draw a circle around *listening* and *confidentiality*. Those two points are especially important.

The following items could be added to Fleischer's list:

◆ *Relationship with parish.* Is our group part of the adult faith-formation program? independent but operating with the express approval of the pastor? not a parish-based group?

◆ *New members.* Will we let new members join us once we have begun the six weeks of discussions?

Agree on housekeeping.

◆ *When will we meet?*

◆ *How often will we meet?* Meeting weekly or every other week is best if you can manage it. William Riley remarks, "Meetings once a month are too distant from each other for the threads of the last session not to be lost" *(The Bible Study Group: An Owner's Manual).*

◆ *How long will meetings run?*

◆ *Where will we meet?*

◆ *Is any setup needed?* Christine Dodd writes that "the problem with meeting in a place like a church hall is that it can be very soul-destroying," given the cold, impersonal feel of many church facilities. If you have to meet in a church facility, Dodd recommends doing something to make the area homey *(Making Scripture Work).*

◆ *Who will host the meetings?* Leaders and hosts are not necessarily the same people.

◆ *Will we have refreshments?* Who will provide them? Don Cousins and Judson Poling make this recommendation: "Serve refreshments if you like, but save snacks and other foods for the end of the meeting to minimize distractions" *(Leader's Guide 1).*

◆ *What about child care?* Most experienced leaders of Bible discussion groups discourage bringing infants or other children to adult Bible discussions.

Agree on leadership. You need someone to facilitate—to keep the discussion on track, to see that everyone has a chance to speak, to help the group stay on schedule. Rena Duff, editor of the newsletter *Sharing God's Word Today,* recommends having two or three people take turns leading the discussions.

It's okay if the leader is not an expert on the Bible. You have this book, and if questions come up that no one can answer, you can delegate a participant to do a little research between meetings. Perhaps someone on the pastoral staff of your parish could offer advice. Or help may be available from your diocesan catechetical office or a local Catholic institution of higher learning.

It's important for the leader to set an example of listening, to draw out the quieter members (and occasionally restrain the more vocal ones), to move the group on when it gets stuck, to get the group back on track when the discussion moves away from the topic, and to restate and summarize what the group is accomplishing.

Bible discussion is an opportunity to experience the fulfillment of Jesus' promise "Where two or three are gathered in my name, I am there among them" (Matthew 18:20). Put your discussion group in Jesus' hands. Pray for the guidance of the Spirit. And have a great time exploring God's word together!

Suggestions for Individuals

Y ou can use this booklet just as well for individual study as for group discussion. While discussing the Bible with other people can be a rich experience, there are advantages to reading on your own. For example:

◆ You can focus on the points that interest you most.
◆ You can go at your own pace.
◆ You can be completely relaxed and unashamedly honest in your answers to all the questions, since you don't have to share them with anyone!

My suggestions for using this booklet on your own are these:

◆ Don't skip the "Questions to Begin." The questions can help you as an individual reader warm up to the topic of the reading.
◆ Take your time on the "Questions for Careful Reading" and "Questions for Application." While a group will probably not have enough time to work on all the questions, you can allow yourself the time to consider all of them if you are using the booklet by yourself.
◆ After reading the "Guide to the Reading," go back and reread the Scripture text before answering the "Questions for Application."
◆ Take the time to look up all the parenthetical Scripture references in the introduction, the Guides to the Readings, and the other material.
◆ Since you control the pace, give yourself plenty of opportunities to reflect on the meaning of Romans for you. Let your reading be an opportunity for these words to become God's words to you.

Bibles

The following editions of the Bible contain the full set of biblical books recognized by the Catholic Church, along with a great deal of useful explanatory material:

- ◆ The Catholic Study Bible (Oxford University Press), which uses the text of the New American Bible
- ◆ The Catholic Bible: Personal Study Edition (Oxford University Press), which also uses the text of the New American Bible
- ◆ The New Jerusalem Bible, the regular (not the reader's) edition (Doubleday)

Books

- ◆ Raymond E. Brown, S.S., "Letter to the Romans," in *An Introduction to the New Testament* (New York: Doubleday, 1997), 559–584.
- ◆ Brendan Byrne, S.J., *Romans* Sacra Pagina Series 6 (Collegeville, MN: Liturgical Press, 1996).
- ◆ Giuliana Pelucchi, *Blessed Gianna Beretta Molla: A Woman's Life, 1922–1962* (Boston: Pauline Books & Media, 2002).
- ◆ William E. Phipps, *Amazing Grace in John Newton: Slave-Ship Captain, Hymnwriter, and Abolitionist* (Macon, GA: Mercer University Press, 2001).

How has Scripture had an impact on your life? Was this booklet helpful to you in your study of the Bible? Please send comments, suggestions, and personal experiences to Kevin Perrotta, General Editor, Trade Editorial Department, Loyola Press, 3441 N. Ashland Ave., Chicago, IL 60657.